Author, Mark Jennings calls time on a truth that has been hidden from the public for more than half a century. Born and raised in South London, Mark recalls his past in detail with a unique and engaging writing style which allows the reader to imagine that they are right there, looking over his shoulder despite the lack of direct influence from his father, Bobby Moore, Mark's life has been dominated by sports. Not only has he enjoyed sports immensely, but they also helped him get through the darkest and most challenging times. Join him on his journey of self-discovery. It's an incredible ride that you'll want to stay on to the end.

I dedicate *Secret Son of a Legend* to Terrie Holsgrove, who unfortunately passed away on 15th December, 2021. For the last two years of her life Terrie battled with cancer, although she had been ill for at least three years prior to that. Terrie was just 19 and I was 23 when we first met. We fell deeply in love with one another and became partners. It was not long before Terrie moved into my Mum's home with me, in Southfield, our relationship continued to blossom. We went on to buy a two-bedroom house in Kent. By this time, Terrie was pregnant with our first son, Grant, and a year later we had a second child, Adam. Terrie and I had our own little family, something that she had always wanted.

Terrie was proud of the way that we brought up our two boys. She was a very good Mum, partner and Grandmother to her Grandchildren. She idolised them all and spent as much time as she could with us. Family meant everything to her, she was also a giver in life and tried to help someone if she could. Terrie liked her puzzle and crossword books. When the game, *Tomb Raider*, came out we enjoyed playing this game together. We played this game for hours on end and continued to play other puzzle games together for many years. We took the kids everywhere, for walks in Battersea Park at the weekends, with our dog, Dolly. Terrie will always be deeply missed by me, her family and her friends.

Mark Jennings

SECRET SON OF A LEGEND

Autobiography

AUSTIN MACAULEY PUBLISHERS™

LONDON • CAMBRIDGE • NEW YORK • SHARJAH

A CIP catalogue record for this title is available from the British Library.

ISBN 9781398478978 (Paperback)
ISBN 9781398478985 (ePub e-book)

www.austinmacauley.com

First Published 2023
Austin Macauley Publishers Ltd®
1 Canada Square
Canary Wharf
London
E14 5AA

I'd like to thank my friend, Nichola Robinson, for all the hard work and the commitment that she has shown in supporting me with my writing. I would also like to take this opportunity to thank Austin Macauley Publishers for helping me through the process of getting my manuscript to publication ready for pubic read and understand my life in great depth.

Table of Contents

Foreword

Something that we all own and keep are our memories. We hold and cherish the best ones for our entire lives, share them with the people that we love and think about them in times of need. Hurtful and painful memories are often best forgotten, though they always remain a part of us. They serve an important purpose, as warnings and as reminders of past mistakes. They help us to avoid future hurt or situations that could create difficulty.

Memories have the ability to change us. They hold important knowledge about our lives, personal attributes and traits and help us to make sense of who we are. Memories of the same events can be different to other people. After all, we each see with our own eyes. My memories have helped me to make sense of my past and to realise that, despite the best efforts of certain people to make me forget, Bobby Moore is my father. Furthermore, he was frequently in my life as a small boy, also during my teens. I never felt as if I was missing a father. Now I have come to realise it's because he was there. Maybe not as 'Dad' but he was in my life nonetheless.

The recollections of the emotional trauma that I suffered as a child have been painful to revisit. The feelings are still very raw, and at times, they have been difficult to write about. Contrarily, my memories about Bobby have all been a delight to think about. Revisiting those times has made me realise that they were fun, loving moments and I will always treasure them. This journey has helped me to learn even more about myself. Until I started writing, I had not realised how much sport has featured in my life, or how I used sport to overcome the difficult times. Everyone has their own version of past events. I have written mine with honesty and in as much depth as possible.

Life in Brixton

I made my entrance into the world on 3 April 1964 in South London Hospital, just opposite Clapham Common. I was the first child of 23-year-old Maureen Jennings. My first home was with Mum and her parents, Charlie and Rose Jennings. Families lived very close to each other in those days, and most of my family lived in Brixton. Way before my birth, in the fifties, much of the family lived together in one big house that belonged to my great-grandmother, Marjorie Frohock. The house was situated just off of Brockwell Park, on the Dulwich side. Grandad Charlie and Nan Rose lived there, as well as Aunt Ciss, her husband Ernie Shenstone, Tommy Frohock and all of the other sisters were there, too. Even Grandad's brother, Arthur. They all lived in the same house! Nan and Grandad didn't stay at the big house forever. When they moved out of the family house, they remained in Brixton and set up home in Brighton Terrace with Mum. I didn't have anyone to call dad, but as a small child, I never really noticed because I had lots of other family members to love and take care of me.

We lived in a two-bedroom, top floor council flat in Trinity Gardens, which was situated just off of Brixton High Street. The entrance to our road, Brighton Terrace, was opposite the big Woolworths store. On the right side of the end of the road, there was a tobacco shop. Here people could purchase cigars, cigarettes, pipes and pipe tobacco. The pipes were displayed on a stand and the cigars were in boxes on shelves. I remember going into that shop one time to exchange a load of old pennies, which I had been saving up in a glass sweet jar, for the new decimal money. On the right side of the road, about a hundred yards away, was a bingo hall with red painted walls and a huge red star centred above it. This place was a social hub for many of the local women, including Nan Rose. A little further along Brighton Terrace, on the left, there were flats which were rented out by Brixton Council. They were three storeys high with a flat either side of the stairwell. Stairs led to the main entrance of the building and the flats lined the left side of the street right up to Trinity Gardens. To the right of these flats, there were a couple of old people's council flats, followed by the houses in Trinity Gardens. The best way to describe the road layout is as a 'P' shape, with Trinity Gardens being the top part of the P. Trinity Gardens was known as 'The Square' to the local kids.

The Square was a safe and friendly place to live. Residents left their doors unlocked and open, and people would always be going in and out of each other's homes. Kids played outside together every day. As the place name suggests, there was a square in front of the flats where myself and the other kids congregated and played cricket against a tall post, as well as other games like run-outs. In this game, we had to split up into two teams. One team would guard the pole and search for the opposition, whilst the other team would go and hide, then make attempts to touch the pole without getting caught.

At the back of the flats, there were communal gardens. Our front room overlooked those gardens. We were not allowed to play in them under any circumstances. But we ignored that and used the garden's bushes to hide from one another and evade capture. I really loved to play that game. It was a firm favourite of all of us. We used to jump off of the sheds that ran along the side of the flats and hang over the gardens. I was about five years old when I jumped down from the sheds for the first time. Nobody told me how to do it and I didn't bend my legs and arms when I landed on the ground below. Well, you can imagine the pain that I was in at that time!

There were some very high, iron railings that the smaller kids could fit between. One day, a boy had become too big to squeeze through so he tried to climb over them instead. The ends of each railing were decorated with very sharp spikes which he unfortunately fell onto. One of the spikes pierced his stomach and the poor boy had to go to hospital for treatment. Another unfortunate boy suffered a broken arm when he fell off of a very high wall. One of the older boys owned a set of golf clubs. On one occasion, he took a swing of his club and accidentally caught the boy standing closely behind him. I'm not sure if that accident caused the injured boy to lose his eye or not, but it was quite a bad injury.

There was a small green right in front of the flats. A foot-high brick wall separated the grass from the pavement. We were daring enough to jump head first over it and then roll onto the grass. Us kids were fearless! We would often sit in groups on the wall or the grass outside the flats. It was good social space, but it was also the scene of scraps from time-to-time, and when I was about six years old, I got my first taste of that. It was with another young boy who was around my age. We were both in the centre of the grass, and all of the other kids were either standing around us or sitting on the wall. Then someone shouted, "Fight!" and the other boy threw me down roughly onto the grass. That was a move that he had learned from the older boys. The altercation was over quickly, and it was the only fight that I ever had whilst I was living at Trinity Gardens.

I learned how to ride my first bike in the square. It had stabilisers on the back wheel when I had my first accident. I was riding it down Brighton Terrace when I lost control by going too fast. I didn't have time to break and slammed into the wall next to me. I was screaming in pain and instinctively touched my head. When I looked at my hand, it was covered in blood. Mum came to my aid when she heard my screams, and I got taken to hospital in an ambulance. Once at the hospital, it was discovered that I had also broken my collarbone. My head was mended with three stitches. As the nurse finished stitching my head, the curtain was pulled back. Mum was standing there with Bobby. Bobby's face had dropped seeing me the way that I was. I thought that he looked sad and concerned. The nurse put my arm in a sling and told Mum that I had to keep it on for some time. We left the hospital together, and Bobby drove us home. Us kids were always getting cuts and bruises, but we just got on with it. Play back then was often very rough, and tumble and accidents like these were not uncommon. They were a part of normal life.

In the sixties, parents didn't supervise their kids like they do now. The only time that Nan Rose and Mum came to look for me was when I had a pedal car and took it out of the square. When they caught up with me in Brixton High Street, they were not amused! I always wanted to be outside, whatever the weather. It was raining one particular day and I really wanted to go and play. Aunt Ciss was visiting and I can remember pleading with her and Mum because they were refusing to let me out in the rain. My aunt took pity and gave in eventually. She said, "Put this on." It was a grey plastic anorak with a hood. I felt silly wearing it because it covered me right down to my feet and the other kids were all outside in their t-shirts or jumpers. But I didn't protest about it because I was out playing, and that's what really mattered.

Mum and I were very close for the duration of the time that we lived with Nan Rose. During the hot summer months, Mum and I enjoyed going to

Brockwell Park Lido. It had been open since 1937 and was built to replace the natural public bathing ponds. There were diving boards and wet changing rooms so that swimmers could change in and out of their swimwear. People didn't tend to travel very far to swim. They just used the pool that was closest to them or in their borough.

When I was indoors at Nan's, I often played alone. I had a Cadbury's chocolate tin which I kept my plastic toy soldiers in. I had quite a collection and liked to set them up all around the front room, then try to knock them down with a rolled up sock. We had a green sofa that was up against the wall in the front room. I would pull it away from the wall slightly, place pillows on the top to close the gap and make a roof, then use a blanket to make a door. I would set up camp inside and play with my toys for hours on end. After I had come home from nursery or from Brockwell Primary School, Mum or Nan put the television on for me. I liked to watch it whilst lying next to the fire.

Most of the films at that time featured cowboys and Indians or some kind of war. Television influenced our outside play quite a lot, so it was no surprise that my favourite game was cowboys and Indians. I used to love playing that with my friends around the square. All of the kids had cap guns. When the cap went off, it sounded like a real gun! The arrows that came with bows had rubber tips that would stick to the walls when they were fired. Then there was the spud gun. EVERYONE wanted this gun. When Ben-Hur came onto the big screen, I wanted the Roman outfit. It came with a sword, a shield and body armour, all moulded from grey plastic. It was the full kit! All of the kids went through phases like these. Play then wasn't like today. None of us back then would have wanted to stay at home, playing online with someone they cannot see. When we played, we went outside all day and came home dirty, grazed and tired. It was so much fun; I wish that I could do it all over again.

In the late 1960s, British households started to invest in colour televisions. They were very expensive, but they made viewing much more enjoyable. The screens on the newer televisions were bigger than before and the picture had a sharper image. This made the experience much better. But the best thing about them was being able to watch in colour. It brought a sense of realism, an enhanced feeling like you were actually there. Back then, it was quite a big deal as the majority of people could only afford black and white. The American sci-fi series *Star Trek* was aired on British Television between 12 July 1969 and 15 December 1971. It was a brand new show so all of the lads were eager to watch it. The family of one of the boys that I played with was fortunate to have a colour television. It was in a light wooden cabinet and took pride of place in the front room. The character's mission was 'to explore strange new worlds, to seek out new life and new civilisations, to boldly go where no man has gone before'. A group of us went to the boy's flat which was in the next block along from mine. We all sat on the floor in a half circle, like kids did when they were watching a *Punch and Judy* show. Many people didn't rush out to buy colour televisions. For several years, a lot of programmes were still only available in black and white anyway. The licence fee was £10. Twice the price of the standard black and white TV licence. The choice of channels was very limited too, with only three channels to choose from; BBC 1, BBC 2 and ITV.

When Guy Fawkes Night came around, all of the residents in Trinity Square got together to build a big bonfire out of scrap wood and old furniture. A Guy that had been made by the children was sat on the top of the pyre. In those days, communities were very strong and nobody was a stranger. There was a mix of wealth with well-off and poorer families living next door to each other. But this didn't matter because families liked to come together and share their fireworks on Guy Fawkes Night. Everybody would stand together around the bonfire, which was very big and impressively tall. Kids made their Guys using old clothes which were stuffed with newspaper to give them a body shape. A stuffed balaclava was often used for the head, and there were special Guy Fawkes masks that could be bought to make the face. Mum helped me to get my Guy ready, and I used my old pram to take it out and get some money.

When I returned home, Nan was indoors and she came to the front door. I could instantly tell by her facial expression that she was not happy. I was unsure of the situation and crept in quietly, almost on tiptoes. Nan closed the door behind me and bent down to my level with her face up close to mine. Looking right into my eyes, she said, "We do not beg in this family." That was the end of it. We had a fairly big coat cupboard in the hall. That's where the pram was also kept, to one side of the coat hooks. I put the Guy in there, but after a couple of days or so, it was gone. I suspect that Nan had disposed of it. That was the first and last time that I ever built a Guy. Nan Rose was a proud lady and she had good morals, which she succeeded in passing down to me. She had taught me never to beg for anything.

The Trinity Arms was a traditional South London pub situated in the north-eastern corner of the square. It was on the end of a terrace of Victorian houses.

All of the buildings on the terrace were decorated with stucco rendering on the ground floor that resembled masonry blocks, yellow bricks on the first floor, with double hung sliding sash windows that were decorated with beautiful architraves. The pub's outside space was lit with ornate iron lanterns that hung above the doors. At night, the pub would always be heaving, and it was a regular meeting place for many local people. When parents were in the pub, us kids would stand outside with a glass bottle of Coke and a packet of crisps. In those days, the crisp packet was full to the top, not half empty like they are today. When the main door was opened, thick tobacco smoke would bellow out and engulf anyone who was standing nearby. The smell of cigars permeated the air mixed with the sickly sweet scent of stale beer.

Arguments and fighting were rare. The men that survived and came back from World War II had already had enough of death and destruction and just wanted to live their lives in peace, so that's what they did. War had affected every family in one way or another. The sixties were one of the more peaceful times, although there was still a lot of change going on around us. The Victoria Line was being extended right into the heart of Brixton, and it was completed in 1971. We could tell the time by hearing the chimes from the big clock at Brixton Town Hall. We could hear it clearly from the front room and, annoyingly sometimes, from our beds at night. We always knew what time it was.

I loved my Nan and Grandad. They both lived with us until Grandad started to see another woman behind my nan's back. I was very young when he moved out, but I would go to my grandad's place at the weekends and sleep over. Nan was heartbroken when they divorced and Grandad married another woman called Hilda. Nan had idolised him and never went into a relationship with anyone else. She loved Grandad until the day that she died. My Aunt Ciss told me that, when they had all lived together in the big house, Nan would lean over Grandad endearingly whilst he was sitting in his chair and say, "You need anything, Char?" My aunt found that very funny because he didn't reply. He would just look at her!

Nan Rose was passionate about bingo. She went along regularly to the Front Line to play it. Due to post-war regeneration, many people from the Caribbean moved into Brixton, and they would also be down the Front Line playing on the 'clicks'. It was a popular pastime for all. Nan said that she used to win her holiday money playing bingo. But she also had a good job as she worked as a civil servant with Aunt Ciss. Mum would take me along to the Front Line with her when it was time to fetch Nan home. But Nan never wanted to leave! Mum would be shouting to get her attention from the doorway, but nobody took any notice of her calls. I used to think that it was quite amusing. Sometimes at the weekend, my aunts and uncles would come to my nan's flat to play cards. They would sit around the big wooden dining table in the front room and smoke cigarettes. The smoke haze hung in thick, white bands in the room. Everyone smoked in those days. I can remember being tall enough for my head to peep over the top of the table, and I would look in awe at the stacks of old One Penny coins that everyone had on show in front of them.

Nan Rose was very traditional, almost Victorian in her ways. She dressed very smartly, unless she was in the kitchen where she would don a pinafore over her dress. We spent a lot of time together rolling pastry out on the kitchen table to make pies and other savoury bakes. She owned jelly moulds in various shapes and sizes and would often encourage me to make the jellies myself. Being allowed to boil the kettle and pour the hot water over the jelly cubes made me feel quite grown up. I loved to stir them around with a wooden spoon, watching them get smaller and smaller until they had completely dissolved away. Then came the impatient wait for the jelly to set. It only took a few hours, but in that short space of time, the anticipation really built up. Once the jelly was ready, I swiftly turned the mould upside down onto a plate and then tentatively lifted it away to watch the jelly slip out. I remember how accomplished I felt when I saw the jelly there in all of its wobbly glory. Nan would always congratulate me for doing such a good job.

When the kitchen table wasn't being used for cooking, Nan kept her tea making things and the butter dish neatly displayed. She always had real butter. The teapot was green, and it was covered by a knitted tea cosy to keep the tea warm whilst it brewed and the sugar was kept in a cut glass bowl. Nan Rose was very psychic. She read people's fortunes using a regular deck of playing cards, and those who had their fortunes read said that she was very good at it. They would come over to her flat for their readings. However, they would only hear about the good predictions. Nan always kept any bad news to herself.

I went shopping with Nan on a pretty regular basis. Most of the time, we went together without any other company, though Mum came along sometimes too. Brixton High Street was very popular in the 1970s and families would travel by bus and train to Brixton to shop because most things could be bought there. Electric Avenue is a street in Brixton which was built in the 1880s. It was the first UK market street to be lit by electric lights. When I was a child, the elegant Victorian canopies that jutted out from the buildings were still there. Each shop's goods were displayed underneath and would-be buyers could walk around, up close, even picking the items up to look at them if they wanted to. Everything of higher value was displayed on a wall behind the shop counter or in the window directly below it. Electric Avenue was well known for its butchers and fishmongers. Nan bought fish from there every week.

As a small child, I was right into Action Man figurines and especially enjoyed looking at the new Action Man stuff that was for sale. Nan Rose indulged me by buying me different outfits for my Action Man. I had several types such as German officer costumes and a frogman that I could play in the bath with. That one came with a small tube that was attached to the wetsuit. When I blew air down it, bubbles came out of the helmet, just like a real diver's. Thunderbirds was a children's 1960s British puppet series that was first shown on television from September 1965 to December 1966. I loved to watch it so Nan bought me Thunderbird 2. Inside the body, there was another toy, Thunderbird 4. I had some great toys back then.

Nan and I both enjoyed spending quality time together. I must have been the apple of her eye, for she was attentive of me in every way and made me feel very loved. Life was pretty good, and all of my family made sure that I had everything that I needed. But Mum was a taker in life rather than a giver. I had a Lloyds Bank account opened up for me whilst we were living with Nan. Every week, £1 had been deposited into the account and the savings were built up to £13. Mum withdrew the money that had been saved for me and bought carpets for the entire flat. That's how much £13 was worth then.

Even though Grandad Charlie and Nan Rose had separated, I still saw Grandad on a regular basis. Mum and I always got picked up by Grandad in his car and driven to his home for Sunday dinner. When we arrived at Grandad and Hilda's bungalow, Mum and I would go into the front room, which had three chairs and a two-seater sofa. If it was wintertime, Hilda would prepare tea and coffee and have the room warmed up with the gas fire ready for our arrival. Once Grandad had put the car away into the garage, he would join us and have a chat with Mum before going out to pick some fresh vegetables for dinner. There was a vegetable plot and greenhouse down the right side of the garden. Grandad went out to get them on his own because he knew which vegetables were ripe for picking. I never helped him, but I liked to go to the conservatory window and watch him from there. Once he had selected what he needed, he brought the vegetables to the kitchen for Hilda to clean and prepare along with the rest of the food. Hilda would have already begun some of the preparations early in the morning before our arrival. A typical Sunday dinner consisted of roast chicken or beef, roasted potatoes and vegetables such as peas, broccoli, carrots and greens. I never liked greens so Hilda kindly omitted them from my plate if she was serving dinner.

We dined using the silver cutlery that was kept in the top drawer of a cabinet next to the dining table which seated six people. Grandad always sat at the head of the table. I had my place next to him on the left and Mum sat opposite me on the right. Before he sat down with us, Grandad always helped Hilda to bring the food from the kitchen which was right next to the dining room, so they didn't have to bring it very far. Grandad carried the meat in, which was on a large China plate. He placed it on the table in front of him whilst Hilda brought the rest of the meal in on separate China plates. The carving knives were kept in the cabinet drawer with the dining cutlery. Grandad liked to get them out of the drawer and then stand over the meat, sharpening them. I used to watch the steel glinting and flashing as the blades were drawn against one another. It was quite an impressive and ceremonious act. Grandad took a lot of pride in doing that, cutting portions of and placing them onto all of our dinner plates. Mum and Hilda shared out portions from the other serving plates.

The food always tasted really good, and I couldn't wait to tuck into it. Once the main course was finished, Hilda cleared all of the plates from the table and took them into the kitchen, and on her return, she brought a dessert. Sometimes jam roly-poly with custard or apple pie. Hilda made them herself, and they were delicious. She was a good cook. Mum liked to help Hilda and loved to be around Grandad. It was as if she was a little girl again in his company. After dinner, we often went out to walk dinner off. We walked together to the Glade where there was a large field. Hilda liked to bring two apples, one for each of the horses that were kept there.

When we returned to the bungalow, we went into the conservatory. There were four armchairs in there which faced the garden area so that their occupants could enjoy the view. If it was a nice day, we used to sit in the garden. There was a goldfish pond right in front of the conservatory, and I enjoyed watching the fish swim in and out of the pond plants. Grandad loved to keep the garden in neat order and I sometimes helped him to cut the lawn. I had fun doing that because he had a petrol mower that he sat on and drove around the gardens, which were quite large, so he needed a cordless mower to get the job done. I also helped Grandad to collect all of the leaves that had fallen. Mum and I always stayed for the full day, rather than just a few hours. Before we left with Grandad to go home, we both said our goodbyes to Hilda and thanked her for having us. I found those days to be very relaxing and liked very much to be with my family. I didn't like going home, even though I knew that I had to. I found leaving hard when the time came.

Bobby

One of my most vivid memories from my early childhood happened when I was about five years old and living with Nan Rose. Ted's son, Edward, would often make visits to Nan Rose's flat. Sometimes his friend Bobby would be with him. I was sleeping on the sofa when they came in, and I was woken up by Edward. Bobby was with Edward on this occasion, and I instinctively put my arms out to hug Bobby. He quickly said, "We don't do that, we shake hands." With that, Bobby firmly put his hand out to shake mine. Before the handshake, Bobby always picked me up when he saw me, but now, it seemed it was the time for more formal greetings! In my family, we have always hugged to greet each other, and I think that this is the reason why this memory has always stuck strongly with me. It felt strange, almost awkward and out of the ordinary.

Mum was also good friends with Bobby, and I remember spending time with them both, going out to shows. I recall going to a couple of shows that were held at the Royal Albert Hall. On 27 November 1969, we went together to watch the Miss World pageant. I didn't need to use opera glasses to see clearly because our seats were just behind the judge's, a few rows from the front of the stage. I watched the whole show intently and remained entertained throughout. The contestants all wore pleasant smiles, which I thought were directed towards me at first. But I realised in the end that they were actually smiling at Bobby, though I never knew why at the time.

We went together to another show at the Royal Albert Hall the following year in 1970. This time, we saw flamenco dancers, and we were much further away from the stage. We had to climb stairs to get to our seats and were given opera glasses, which helped me to see the dancers better. I remember being dressed very smartly for the occasion. The venue was packed solid by the time that Mum, Bobby and I arrived. The lights had already gone down and the show was about to start. We had watched flamenco dancers on our holidays in

Spain together so it didn't feel out of the ordinary to go to watch them at the Royal Albert Hall.

An event that I attended in my early twenties sparked memories of those previous experiences. Steve, a very good friend of mine at the time, lived in Stockwell. He had a spare ticket to go and see Kenny G play the saxophone at the Royal Albert Hall. The ticket cost a fiver and I took up Steve's offer to go. We sat in seats halfway up the auditorium. Memories of the past came flooding back to me as we sat watching the show. I remembered my times spent there with Mum and Bobby, even where we sat on those occasions. I was taken right back to those times. Steve and I had a good night and enjoyed it very much. Not only for the show but also for the memories. I didn't tell Steve that I had been there before. I kept it to myself.

Sometime during the same year, I remember going to the Brixton Academy in Stockwell Road, London, to watch the first showing of *Planet of the Apes*. Mum and Bobby took me there, and we sat up in the gallery on the left side, facing the big screen. The gallery was known as the 'posh' area and viewers had to pay extra for the better seats. I remember enjoying the evening very much. Bobby had the ability to make me laugh out loud. Mum laughed with us, too. Bobby had charisma and was always a joy to be around. He made me feel safe. We had a great night watching the film together and left the venue feeling really happy.

I remember a summer's day when Mum and I were out with Bobby. We were in an unfamiliar part of London where the road was very wide and there were a lot of people busily walking about. I remember a petrol garage on the corner of the road with apartments above it. They had windows that made the whole building stand out because they had green frames. Bobby drove his car into an entrance that was next to the petrol garage. It went downwards, into an underground carpark. We got out of the parked car and walked up the stairs into the main building. As we walked past the ground floor entrance, there were a couple of porters standing by the doors. We walked past the elevator and went up the stairs. I'm not sure which floor we walked to but it was a lot of stairs. When we reached our floor, we walked to the end of a long corridor. Bobby opened the door, and I was ushered in to a green room. Everything matched; the bed covers, lampshades, curtains. Even the carpets. The shades were different, but they all complimented one another. I went there on a couple of occasions and never forgot its splendour.

Grange Manor Farm

During the sixties, Mum, and maybe also Nan Rose, took me on holidays to a place called the Grange Farm Manor in Chigwell, which was then owned by West Ham United Football Club. Sometimes, we went there in the summer, but there were also occasions where we stayed there at Christmastime too. The Grange was an impressive manor house with a big driveway out front which had an old, abandoned horse stable to the right. As a child, the entrance door looked enormous with white, twin pillars flanking each side. It was certainly an impressive sight to me. The main entrance room was quite a large area and the first thing that people couldn't help but notice was the impressive stairs which started at the right side of the room and spiralled up and towards the left side where it joined with the first floor. There was a gallery on the same floor that looked towards the stairs. Other features of this area were a traditional log fireplace and an old, red leather chair with a little round table which was situated right inside the front door.

The rooms to the right of the main entrance were very large. They had a door on the opposite side that would take you into the next room. There was also a long hall that ran alongside them which led to a much bigger room at the end. The lounge room, which was next to the main entrance, was the place where guests liked to congregate in the afternoons and evening times. It was quite a cosy room with armchairs and small tables. In the afternoon, guests sat in there and enjoyed tea and biscuits. Later on in the day and into the evening, they played cards. But the favourite pastime was Scrabble. The games went on for hours! My mum was a talented player and she always took part. It wasn't the largest room in the house. However, it was the room with the most energy. It had a warm and welcoming feeling, like being back at home in my own front room.

There was a huge, brass gong beneath the stairs that was used to let everyone know when food was ready at mealtimes. It had a distinct sound that

26

could be heard in every room of the huge house. All of the kids that stayed there wanted to have a go at beating it. From time-to-time, the lady housekeeper would let us sound the gong so we would all race to be there first to get a chance. I liked to get up early and would always be one of the first down to breakfast. There were lots of options to suit every taste, such as full English breakfast, cereal or fruit. I only ever ate cereal for breakfast. My favourite was Weetabix with milk and two boiled eggs with a couple of slices of bread.

I used to get up early in the morning, which meant that I was one of the first people ready for breakfast. There were only a few people in the dining room. I would first stand by the door and peep in to see if there was anyone in there that I recognised. I didn't like to sit alone. There were adults in there that I knew well. One was a beautiful woman called Tina. She was Bobby's wife. Another recognisable face was Bobby's good friend Martin Peters. He used to come on holidays with us a lot, too. As soon as Tina saw me, she would beckon me over with her hand to sit next to her. She was a kindly woman, and I enjoyed our conversations.

A magnificent Christmas tree was set up in a room at the end of the house. It was so tall that it almost touched the ceiling. There were many presents placed underneath the decorated tree, however, the room was void of any other kind of decoration or furniture. The rest of the house had paintings on the walls, but there were none here. The floor was covered in vinyl rather than carpet, and it felt cold. Christmas decoration could be found throughout other parts of the house, including big socks which were hung up on the fireplaces of the rooms that we were sleeping in. They would be filled with nuts, pears, tangerines and maybe a small toy. On Christmas Eve, glasses of milk and biscuits were laid out for Santa Claus. They were put onto a small round table next to the fire in the main entrance.

At night, I can remember sneaking out of my room to sit on the stairs with other kids hoping to catch a sight of Santa, but of course, we never did. We just ended up falling asleep and being carried back to bed. My mum didn't carry me. Bobby carried Roberta and me back to our beds. I remember our times at Grange Farm Manor feeling very festive, with the grounds deep in snow and all of the bushes and trees hanging heavy with it too. When I looked out at the garden through the big sash windows, it was a beautiful sight. Everything was white. One time, I noticed a frog sitting on a round stone base that was in the

27

centre of the garden. The frog really stood out against the white background. I could spend ages looking out of the window. It was like another world at the grange. It was so far removed from my life at home.

For entertainment, us kids played 'run-outs' in the house, which provided ample places to hide seeing as it had three floors. I would hide in the library room which was at the end of the hall to the right. The library had books on every shelf, up to the ceiling. The carpet was very thick, and the wooden chairs were old and covered in leather. It looked like something out of a film.

The room had a smell of its own. Aged and little bit musty. A girl that I was very good friends with would hide behind those chairs with me, trying not to make a sound, but we couldn't stop ourselves from sniggering at each other. We got caught every time by the other kids that were searching for us. Memories of these times are some of my most favourite, and I often think back to them with a lot of fondness.

An outside swimming pool and tennis courts could be found in the grounds behind the house. In the summertime, Mum and I went to the pool every day and I learned how to swim there. To get to the swimming pool, we walked along the right side of the garden and up the stone steps. The pool was directly opposite and the tennis courts were to the right. At the far end of the pool, there were two very small changing rooms; one for men and one for women. Bobby was always about at Grange Manor Farm. I remember him wearing a thick, cream-coloured cardigan, which was fashionable at the time. When the days were hot, the men enjoyed sitting together in deckchairs in the garden, next to the old greenhouse that was attached to the back of the main building.

To the right of the manor, there was a wooded area with tall trees. We knew full well that we were forbidden to enter it without adult supervision. However one day, a group of us kids decided to ignore the rules and go exploring together. Even though it was around midday and the sky was lit with brilliant sunshine, it started to get a bit dark as we entered the trees. The woods were cool and smelled earthy. We hadn't walked that far when we came across an abandoned swimming pool. It was still full of water but covered in dead leaves. It looked as if it had not been used for a very long time. There was a young girl with us who liked to talk a lot and was very knowledgeable. She always seemed to have the answers. We were like best friends when we were on our holidays. She told us an unnerving story about someone drowning in the pool, and we never mustered the courage to go there again. I don't know whether she had made it up or not. It was a convincing and scary story at the time either way!

Festive Season at Home

If we didn't stay at the grange over the festive period, we stayed at home with Nan Rose in Brixton, and Mum's family would come to visit. Twelve nights before Christmas, Mum and I decorated the tree with Nan's decorations which had been cherished and well looked after for many years. The tree was decorated with a string of electric fairy lights that shone like gems, and it was topped with an angel. I liked to hang the delicate glass baubles on the branches myself. The bow-topped presents were under the tree during the run up to the big day and this added to my excitement. On Christmas Day, Nan and I woke up early, and Nan got straight on with things that needed to be done. Like a lot of children, the excitement and anticipation of the day made it hard for me to sleep. But I was enthusiastic and the tiredness didn't affect me. I remember waking with a happy smile, knowing that the day had come. I opened my presents as soon as I woke up in the morning. I got up before Mum and leapt out of bed and put on my blue dressing gown. I wasn't expected to wait for anyone else. One of my best presents was in a very large box. As I tore the wrapping paper off, I could see part of a train set emerging. It was a Hornby train set. The best of the best. Nan had already moved her bed over so that I could set it out. It came with a massive red board that had been laid on Nan's bedroom floor. It was electric and came with a speed box to make the trains faster or slower. I spent hours playing with it, and it gave me a lot of joy. To my delight, I also got a cherry-coloured boy's Raleigh bike. The majority of kids in those days were fortunate enough to receive presents but some that I knew were not as lucky. They didn't get anything. Nan liked to be organised and she knew how to get all of the tasks completed with military precision so that the meal would be ready and on the table in a timely manner. I used to enjoy helping Nan to lay the table with Christmas crackers, which contained colourful paper hats at every place setting. We always had the traditional turkey Christmas dinner with all of the trimmings. The smell in the flat was divine. Even though I had eaten breakfast in the morning, it wasn't very long before the wonderful cooking aromas that emanated from the kitchen forced my hunger to return.

By midday, the visitors started to arrive; Jean and Ted, Aunt Ciss and Uncle Ernie. Ted and Uncle Ernie liked to make hats out of newspaper and they were very good. Christmas pudding and steaming hot custard was always served for dessert. Nan liked to do things the traditional way so she put a sixpence inside the pudding, which I always managed to get! After dinner was finished, the table was cleared and cleaned, and then the adults played cards for small amounts of money. Nan had a small drinks cabinet which was only opened for a special occasion. Christmas Day was one of those occasions. The telly stayed off. The men went to the Trinity Arms for a pint after dinner. There were occasions where Mum and I went with Grandad Charlie to visit his brother's home, which was close by as he also lived in Brixton. We stayed and the adults had drinks together. I was allowed a Snowball. It was yellow in colour and creamy. I liked it very much. It was the only time that I was allowed to drink, but I did take sips from the sherry and Martini bottles on the quiet...

On New Year's Eve, I stayed in with my family; Mum, Nan, aunts, uncles and Mum's cousins. It was a joyous occasion and everyone was always in good spirits. Like Christmas Day, the men went to the pub for a drink. They were back again before midnight to sing songs together. When midnight came, the adults all stood in a circle, holding hands. I remember them singing songs like *Knee's Up Mother Brown* and the *Hokey Cokey*. Everyone was very happy shaking their arms and legs in and out. They were great times that I had with my family. As tradition dictated, the Christmas tree and decorations were always taken down on the twelfth night.

Visiting Great-Aunt Dolly

Great-aunt Dorothy lived in a town called Maidstone in Kent. She was Nan Rose's sister. Dolly, as she preferred to be called, lived on a long piece of sloping land in a bungalow. The garden went down in stages and at the bottom there was a large caravan. Me, Mum and Nan Rose would sleep there when we stayed over. It was adequate, but nothing like home. It didn't have electricity, or a toilet, but I loved staying there! Nan Rose used to sleep in the spare room at the bungalow. But there were two rooms in the caravan; Mum and I would each have a room and sleep there. They were pretty good times. Mum and I would often sit in the caravan together and amuse ourselves with painting activities. Mum was very talented at it, and she taught me how to become skilled at it by doing painting by numbers. On dark evenings, we would paint by gas light. I can remember the hissing sound and how the bright, white light of the mantle would create shadows on the walls.

Away from the caravan, there was endless farmland and woodland to explore. One time, I went into an apple field with my mum's cousin's kids in the dark! We got caught by the farmer who started to come at us shouting so we all ran away, leaving a trail of dropped apples! But what fun we had, such an adrenaline rush! We didn't dare tell our parents for fear of a stern reprimand. Uncle Ernie and I had always been very close. He was very good to me and gave me a lot of his attention. When we were on one of our holidays in Spain, he bought me a Spanish penknife. It was fancy with a pattern finish on the handle, and I took it everywhere with me. We used to visit the English countryside on a regular basis. On this particular occasion, we visited some woodlands in Maidstone, near Aunt Dolly's house. I threw my penknife at a tree from a distance with the intention of it sticking into the bark. But the blade didn't go in and the knife ricocheted off of the tree and fell to the ground which was covered in leaves. I looked and looked for it, but it couldn't be found. It was lost forever, and I was sad about that for a while.

We attended the local church whilst we visited Aunt Dolly. On one occasion, Nan had a black-out whilst sitting right next to me.

Uncle Ernie's Passing

It was 4 January 1971, when I was woken abruptly by the sound of loud knocking. I was in bed at Nan's flat, and it was very early in the morning. Nan answered the door and saw Aunt Ciss standing alone in the doorway crying. Nan asked in a concerned voice what had happened and my aunt replied to her, "It's Ernie – he passed away during the night." I had never seen my aunt so upset and crying before. Tears were rolling down her cheeks, and she was completely inconsolable. It made me feel really sad too because Uncle Ernie had been quite a big influence in my life and he meant a lot to me. Uncle Ernie's passing was my first experience of losing someone that I cared very much for. He cared for me, too.

We had a relationship a bit like father and son, though I looked up to my grandad the most. Uncle Ernie had served in the Navy during the Second World War on an aircraft carrier. He was a well-spoken man with a good temperament. After the war had ended, he returned to his trade as a master stonemason. Some of the things that I remember him making were a marble table and ashtray, a clock and some jewellery. I found a John Player's Navy Cut cigarette box in Aunt Ciss' garden shed. It contained personal items which included a pair of earrings. One had been finished, but the other was still in the stone. At the time of his death, I believe that he was one out of only nine men who were classed as master stonemasons. Skills and trades often die with the person, but items, places or even a name can make memories flood back. The sight of any penknife would make me think of Uncle Ernie.

Holidaying in Spain

I can recall some great family holidays in my early life. Every year, we went to Platja de L'Estartit in Spain and stayed in the same villa. It was like a family tradition. We travelled by plane and then took a coach from the airport. I was always very excited about going on family holidays, and I recall the view of the sea as we approached the resort. As we got nearer, I could see a group of people on the sand watching someone with sun-bleached hair and a golden tan repeatedly kicking a football high on one foot to another and keeping it up for a long time. I smiled when I saw that it was Bobby. I always looked out for him with anticipation. He was such a pleasure to watch and seemed to revel in showing his talent off. Bobby spent a lot of time showing the locals his football skills and also had fun kick-abouts with them.

Mum and I, Nan Rose, Aunt Ciss and her husband Ernie all stayed in a villa which was situated quite close to the beach. The roads were still made of dirt and unfinished back then. Most days, we went down to the beach. Mum and Nan liked to place their deckchairs next to each other and facing the sea. Bobby was there playing football with the locals. He walked over towards us. My aunt jokingly said out loud, "Here comes the German with his blonde hair, blue eyes and golden tan!" Nan Rose and Aunt Ciss looked at each other and giggled because he wasn't German at all. We were all part of one big family holidaying together. But Bobby didn't stay at the villa with us. He, his wife and children were staying at one of the two hotels close by. Bobby would sometimes play with me, helping me to build sandcastles on the beach with my bucket and spade. I also spent a lot of time with Bobby's wife, Tina. I especially loved to be with their daughter, Roberta. She was my best friend and I loved to be around her because she was very intelligent and entertaining to be around. We had a lot of fun conversations together too.

Going out for the evening was treated like a special occasion, and we all dressed up really smart. We always went to a club or a venue where they had entertainment outside. A couple of names that I remember are El Galleon and La Raquetta Tamarin. The clubs that we went to typically had a dance floor surrounded by tables and an outside bar. Flamenco dancers were the most popular entertainment. There were other traditional entertainments to be enjoyed, such as singers or someone playing a Spanish guitar, and there would always be champagne at our table. The nights in Spain were hot so the bottle was sat in a stainless steel bucket filled with lots of ice to keep it chilled. The entertainments lasted until very late in the evening. After the live shows finished, everything was cleared away so that the dance floor was free for people to get up and party until home time.

I vividly remember one occasion when we were all out at a club and Bobby arrived shortly after us. The place started to fill with photographers who were behind him. They surrounded Bobby and started calling out to him whilst clicking away with their cameras. There were many bright flashes from the camera bulbs, and I remember Bobby pushing me behind him. I was made to come out of the way and sit down at the table with my mum. Looking back, we got the VIP treatment whenever we were at those clubs, though at the time I didn't realise as I was just a small boy.

In the shops and at the hotel, there were vending machines where we could buy Spanish matchboxes with pictures of Bull Fighters on them. They were black, and Roberta and I loved collecting them. Mum liked to buy my shoes whilst on holiday in Spain because she said that the quality of the leather was better. If I couldn't have shoes from Spain, we went to Clarks in Brixton High Street instead.

My mother and Bobby were very good friends with a Spanish jeweller who owned a small shop that was close to the beach. We went there from time to time while we were on our holidays together. On one occasion, I was bought a gold signet ring that had the initials MJ carved into it. Mum and I followed Bobby into the shop. A smiling man walked out from behind his counter and then bent down to greet me. The jeweller's face was just a bit higher than mine when Bobby said to me in a hushed playful tone, "Go on, punch him." Without much thought I landed my fist straight on the end of the man's nose! The jeweller retreated and my face dropped for a couple of seconds because I thought that I would be in trouble for actually hitting the man. But Bobby immediately started to laugh, followed by Mum and the jeweller. It must have been a comical scene to behold. Other items were purchased too, such as gold bracelet charms. Mum had lots of them. I remember being presented with a pair of red cherry boxing gloves and a matching boxing bag when we got home. The boxing bag was hung up in the hallway. I really liked that gift and remember playing with the gloves until I could no longer fit my hands in them.

The Big Family Breakdown

At home, there was a massive argument within the family. I vividly remember witnessing Mum shouting loudly at Nan Rose in the kitchen. I was standing in the hallway, out of view, but I could see in through the open doorway. Mum and Nan were having an argument. I heard Nan tell Mum not to go on the planned holiday to Spain with them. I could only see Nan's back and Mum was out of sight further inside the room. Bobby's name was mentioned several times. It was a heated exchange, and Nan shouted back to Mum that she had to get out. She shouted that she didn't want us to live there anymore.

Nan was extremely upset, and I could hear that she was sobbing. Her shoulders were moving up and down. She suddenly slumped forwards and fell sideways off of her chair, then onto the floor with a huge thump. Nan had suffered another blackout. I had never seen Mum shout at Nan in that way before and it made me feel quite scared. I didn't go into the kitchen. I saw Mum move forwards to pick Nan up from the floor. I quietly went back into my bedroom. I never heard any heated arguments between Mum and Nan again.

I had collected many great memories of Spain over the years, but the holiday in 1971 was markedly different from the previous ones. I didn't see Bobby kicking a football about on the beach. Or Tina. We (me, Mum, Nan and Aunt Ciss) stayed in the same villa, but the atmosphere had changed. Even as a small boy, I could sense that there was tension in the air. It was beyond my understanding and I didn't know how to read the situation.

The only other person that I did see was Roberta. I came down the steps at the side of the villa. When I reached the bottom, I saw her standing there with hunched shoulders and slanted eyes. I think that my instinct must have told me that the relationship had changed between us. It didn't feel friendly, and I stopped abruptly in front of her. Roberta was only a few feet in front of me, but we didn't speak a word. We stood there unmoving and looked at each other for a moment, which felt much longer than it actually was. The road outside the villa was wet and muddy with tyre tracks in it as it wasn't tarmacked. Roberta crouched down and picked up a handful of wet mud, then threw it straight at my face! After that, she just ran off. I was left standing there confused, dirty and a little bit upset. I didn't know why my friend would do something like that to me. We had always been so happy in each other's company.

At that pivotal time, my life changed dramatically – and not for the better! Very soon after the mud incident, I was told that I would never be allowed to see my family, or Roberta, again. That hurt me a lot as I felt that we were very close. Uncle Ernie had only passed away recently and I was finding the changes really hard. I had stopped seeing almost all of the people that I loved and cared about, and I felt lost, almost alone. From that time forward, I was only allowed to see Grandad Charlie. He forbade me and Mum from seeing the family, especially the Martin family and the Moore family. But Bobby's name was still mentioned when I visited other family member's houses.

Mum's New Relationship

I turned seven years of age in 1971. Mum started to date a man called David Graves. His family lived in Camberwell, and he worked in a men's boutique. He seemed to be all right at first, but as time went on, he began to show his true colours to me. There was one particular occasion where David came over to Nan Rose's flat in Brixton. I didn't know where Mum or Nan had gone to, and for some reason, he and I were left alone. I was taking a bath when I accidentally defecated in it. David came into the bathroom and immediately saw the stool floating around in my bath water. He pointed at it whilst looking directly at me with cold, staring eyes. He abruptly demanded, "What is that?" I wasn't sure how to respond to his question so I started to laugh nervously. But David didn't find it funny at all! He grabbed the stool out of the water with his bare hand and proceeded to rub it all over me from head to toe. I sat still in shock and absolute silence.

With the shit still smeared on his hands, David stood intimidatingly over me. He had a smug look on his face when he sternly said, "You won't do that again!" Even as a small child, that wicked act made me feel dirty and ashamed. My nan never got to know about this incident. In fact, I didn't utter a word about it to anyone. It was a huge shock to be treated so cruelly, and it left me feeling extremely bewildered and confused. I couldn't understand why David had been so wicked or what I had done to deserve that kind of treatment from him. Up to that point in my life, I'd never been abused. I'd never even received a smack.

Return to the Grange

Mum told me that we were going to the Grange Manor Farm. We were only going for the weekend, which felt unusual to me. Normally, we went for at least a week. David and his niece came too. We arrived on a cold evening and it was dark. We entered the main door and went up the stairs to our allocated rooms on the fourth floor. David looked really agitated, like he didn't want to be there. I noticed, too, that David's niece was very nervous. It was the first time that she had stayed in such a big house, and it was naturally a very unsettling experience.

David's niece and I were escorted into a room and David told us that we would be sharing. Mum and David had their own room next to ours. David's niece was told to look after me because they were going out for the rest of the evening. Mum and David got ready quickly and then came to say goodbye. They made sure that we were in our beds before they left our room and closed the door behind them. There was nobody else around, and it was very quiet in the big house. It certainly had a spooky feeling about it because we were staying in one of what I called the 'attic rooms'. The attic rooms were basic and simply styled. I had never stayed in an attic room before. Every other time that I'd stayed at Grange Manor Farm, we'd slept in the plusher rooms on the first floor.

We were both scared of the dark and left the bedroom light on. Shortly after we had been left alone, I heard a whisper from David's niece, "Mark, I've wet my bed." She asked me if she could share my bed with me. I agreed to her request, and she came over and got in. The poor girl must have been very anxious because she wet my bed a little as well. So we both got up and sat together on the side of the bed. We sat there until Mum and David returned, earlier than we expected. The door opened wide, and David entered the bedroom, followed by Mum. David's face looked hard, as if he was ready for a fight. He demanded us to tell him why we had both gotten up. I explained that the beds were both wet. Before I knew what was happening, David lifted me up to a standing position on the wooden chair that was next to my bed. My face was almost level with David's. He looked to his niece and asked her, only once, why both of the beds were wet. She replied, "I didn't do it."

David was full of rage, and it was all focussed in my direction. He then stared at me into my eyes and asked me if I had wet the beds. I told him that I didn't do it. David slapped me hard across the side of my face with an open hand. Then asked me again, and again. Each time, I replied with the same answer, and each time, I got slapped. David smacked both of my cheeks. This caused me to have tears streaming down my face. I had no choice but to tell David that it was me who had made the beds wet. He wouldn't stop slapping me until I told him what he wanted to hear. David's niece and I were made to sleep in the wet beds that night.

I awoke the following morning and David told me to remove the wet sheets from the beds. I was made to carry them down to the housekeeper and apologise. I said sorry to her whilst holding them up to show them to her. I felt deeply embarrassed and kept my head lowered. I couldn't look her in the eyes. Since Mum and David had returned from their night out, they had faces like thunder. Unsurprisingly, we didn't stay at the house for the full weekend like Mum said we would. We left at around midday and never returned there again. I came to realise recently that they must have had a meeting with Bobby because I overheard some of the later conversations where Bobby was mentioned.

The Bedsit

Mum and I moved out of Nan's flat a short while after our stay at Grange Manor Farm. We went to live in a ground floor room in a big house just off of Tulse Hill. Mum and David were in a committed relationship so David moved with us to our new home. Because we only rented a room, we shared the bathroom and the kitchen area with other residents. The kitchen, which was situated at the back of the house, was nothing like the modern kitchens that we expect now. There was a stand up oven with four burners on the top. An eye-level wall-mounted grill was next to it. The kitchen also contained a small table and a very basic sink. If someone wanted to make a cup of tea, they had to heat a pot of water on one of the burners because there wasn't a kettle. The shared bathroom was on the first floor. Our room was sparsely furnished with two single beds and a table and chairs that we ate our dinner at. We didn't have a television or a telephone.

It was very cramped accommodation with no space to play or anywhere else for me to escape to. I was no longer in my safe zone. Nan's flat had been relatively secure, but once we moved to the new flat, I became extremely vulnerable to David's abusive ways. I used to snore quite loudly at night. David didn't like it and he showed his displeasure through acts of physical violence. In his anger, he would grab my limbs and drag me from the bed. Once on the floor, he would pick me up with both hands and throw me right across the room. He did it with a force so immense that my body hit the wall hard. I owned a Spanish toy guitar which had been hung on the wall. One time, I was flung at the wall so hard that the guitar fell down and hit me on the top of my head. Mum didn't ever intervene when David was bullying or abusing me. He had complete control when it came to rules and discipline. He made me sleep next to him and threatened me not to move or to make a sound. I tried my hardest to keep quiet and still all night, which meant that I never slept properly and was always tired.

I remained at Brockwell School for the whole time that we lived at the bedsit. Mum usually came to collect me at the end of the school day. If she was going to be late, I had to wait for her to arrive in the big hall. If Mum knew that she was going to work late, she told me to go to my Great-aunt Agnes' (Jean) flat. Jean and Ted lived across the road from the school. That worked out okay at first, but they moved, so I had no option but to go to Nan's flat by bus. I was only seven years old, but Mum must have decided that it was okay for me to do that because the bus stops were right outside the school and close to Brighton Terrace.

I had done the bus ride alone several times, but something that happened on the way home one dark evening meant that it would be the last. When I left school, it was already getting very dark outside. I came outside and went down the steps to stand at the bus stop in front of me. I was the only person waiting there so I stood quietly and patiently. As my bus came towards me, I could see its lights on. At that moment, I sensed that someone was behind me so I turned my head to see a very big man approaching. He was wearing an overcoat and a flat cap. I felt the man shove me quite hard so I looked around again and our eyes met. He was looking straight at me. I started to feel very afraid of his presence. As the bus stopped, I noticed all of the people inside, and it made me feel a sense of relief.

I hurried on and sat in a vacant seat that was near to the front of the bus. The big man sat in the seat behind me. It was only a short ride to Brixton High Street. As I neared my stop, I got up and walked towards the back of the bus. The big man did too. Even though I couldn't see him, I could sense him towering behind me. I could feel him trying to grab and nudge me as I staggered hurriedly along the aisle. The other passengers were looking and must have noticed my nervous face and that something was wrong.

In those days, the back of the bus was open so passengers just hop on and off. There was a white pole that went from ceiling to floor which I hung onto. The big man was there too. He started to try to push me off of the bus, but two other men close by intervened and grabbed onto him. I jumped off of the moving bus just before the stop. One of the passengers who was holding the big man shouted out, "It's all right, boy, we've got him!"

I ran as fast as my short legs could carry me, all of the way along Brighton Terrace to Nan's flat. My heart was thumping hard in my chest as I ran up the steps to the front door. As I approached the door, I saw Nan there, wearing her pinny. She was washing down the step with a bucket of water and a mop. I was so relieved to see her standing there. Through gasps of breath, I told Nan what had just happened to me. It obviously scared Nan and the rest of our family too because I was not allowed to go home from school alone for some time afterwards. Grandad Charlie was waiting in his car to bring me to Nan's every day for the rest of the week. After that, Mum picked me up as soon as school finished. It must have been a terrible shock for Mum to think that I could have been taken so easily. Eventually, Mum allowed me to walk home from school to the bedsit because I had the company of some other kids who lived nearby.

It was coming towards the end of the summer and the nights had started to draw in. I went into Brockwell Park with a couple of other boys from school to play football. We stayed there until it became very dark and then, when we came out of the park and started to walk home next to the school, we encountered David coming towards us. I started to fill with feelings of dread. I could see from the look on his face that he was not very happy, and I was certain that he would take that anger out on me somehow. He spitefully snatched my football away from me and ordered me to follow him back to the house.

David marched me straight into the kitchen, called Mum into the room and then strictly instructed her to stand in the corner, facing us both. He ordered me remove my clothes and stand totally naked in the middle of the room. I think that David's intention was to make me feel extremely vulnerable and exposed. It worked. He picked up a large carving knife from the kitchen table and, after looking at me with a cruel grin, he used the knife to stab repeatedly at the ball in quite a frenzied way. I remember the attack making me feel very anxious and scared. Instinct was telling me to run away, but I didn't dare to move.

After he had finished stabbing at the football, David turned his attention onto me again. He hit me all over my body many times with a leather slipper, and Mum was made to remain in the corner and watch. Feeling unable to intervene, she just stood there trembling and crying helplessly. Once he was finished, David ordered me back out of the kitchen. My skin was reddened and raised. It felt very sore and stung for some time afterwards. David's violent acts towards me were sadly not uncommon. It was around that time Nan Rose noticed that I had many bruises on my body, including a bruise that looked like a bite mark on my bottom. She told Grandad what she had seen, but nothing happened to change what was going on. David continued to abuse me.

45

Move to Tooting

We only stayed at the bedsit for a few months before moving on to a flat in Tooting. It was in Trinity Road, about two hundred yards from Tooting Station. Our home was above a photo developing shop. Shops nearby were a butcher's, fruit and veg shop along with a few others. We had a back entrance to our home which could be accessed via an alleyway from the street. There were a lot of steps up to the top flat. We shared a toilet on the first floor with an Irish couple who had two very young children. There was a bath in our kitchen with an Ascot heater above it. That would be highly dangerous by today's standards, but it was completely acceptable then. The front room was next to the kitchen, then there were two bedrooms on the top floor upstairs. One for Mum and David and one for me. We didn't have a toilet in the flat. It was on the first floor, too far away to walk down from the bedrooms. David solved the issue by placing a bucket in the hallway, just outside his bedroom. Every morning, I was expected to carry the bucket down the stairs to the toilet and empty it. I could hear the contents swilling around, and I was glad that the bucket had a lid. It was always filled to the brim and the stench was putrid. It made me gag when I poured the contents away.

Mum and David worked long hours so I was left to my own devices quite a lot. Mum worked in the city at a local sorting office. She had a management role. David started working on building sites. There were many occasions where I was left alone, especially in the summer holidays. There was one day in particular when Mum and David were at work and I had been left to my own devices. It was in the afternoon and I was at the local shops opposite the alleyway. Whilst I was standing there I noticed the presence of a large man near to me, getting closer and closer. I decided to leave the shops and go straight home. I looked behind me and the man was walking fast in my direction. I could see him gathering speed and his eyes were firmly on me so I instinctively ran across the road to the alleyway. I looked around again and the big man was running across the road after me! I turned the corner in the alleyway and ran straight to my front door. When I looked again, the man had turned the corner. I hurried into the opened door and slammed it closed again. I then ran up the stairs and opened my bedroom window to see into the alleyway. The big man was gone. I stayed in the flat for the rest of the afternoon and kept to myself. Looking back, I should have told Mum about it because it was not an isolated incident. I was more aware of my surroundings from that time forward.

Sometimes, I went to Leysdown with David's brother, Fred. We stayed there in a caravan on one of the sites. Other times, I went to David's sister's flat. But there were some summer weekends where I would go with Mum to Tooting Bec Lido. It was one of the oldest open-air swimming pools at the time and had been open since the spring of 1906. It had only taken four months to build. It was an unheated pool so it always felt freezing cold, even on the hotter days. There was sometimes a certain degree of hesitancy about getting into the water. People could be seen loitering around the poolside and testing it with a foot before inching in slowly whilst gasping and shuddering. Others dived from the boards or just jumped in from the side.

We went to enjoy the amenities as a large group of kids as well as parents David never came along with us and that suited me just fine. Once at the pool, we put our towels down so that we could lay on them later on. Mum liked to bring a small radio so that we had something to listen to. We just laid talking to whoever came along with us or went into the pool for a swim. I loved to go swimming, and it was the first sport that I took a serious interest in. I would swim all year around. My friends and I also liked to go to the public swimming pool, and we took up all of the challenges when we went swimming at school. I was awarded for my efforts with many swimming certificates. Even though I wasn't very fast, I still loved to take part in a race. I was very good at swimming distances because I was physically strong and had stamina.

In 1970s, Britain power cuts and blackouts were a fact of life and they occurred frequently. Electricity in our home was supplied on a pay-as-you-go basis. The lights went out if the meter needed to be topped up with coins too. The meter in our home was above the door in the front room. If the lights went out whilst Mum and David were out, I had to search in the dark for the torch, climb a step ladder to reach the electricity meter, put money in the coin slot and hope for the lights to come back on. But they often didn't, and I had to remain in darkness and just wait for the power to return. Power cuts could last for hours!

Living with Grandad

We hadn't been living in Tooting long when Grandad Charlie came to remove me from my mother and David. It was late in the night, about ten or eleven o'clock. We heard loud banging on the front door, which was quite far away from our flat and downstairs. Whoever it was had made it very clear that they wanted immediate attention. The banging was very hard and it was totally unexpected. David went to see who the visitor was whilst Mum and I stayed in the front room. It was an utter surprise when Grandad and his four brothers came in. They spoke threateningly to David about the marks that Nan Rose had seen on my body and Grandad told me to get dressed so that I could go with him. I immediately did what I was told without questioning. Then we left. David was outnumbered and he couldn't do anything about it. Mum didn't say a word. Grandad ushered me into his car and took me home with him. I gladly left that awful place and went to live with him and Hilda.

Grandad Charlie and Hilda lived in Surry in a small, historic village called Little Bookham. The journey to his bungalow led us across a small railway bridge which was only wide enough for one car at a time. This road carried on into the glade. At night, it was very dark because there weren't any street lights. Grandad's bungalow was the first one that we saw. In the seventies, all of the homes on both sides of the road were bungalows. However, as time passed, some of the occupiers renovated them and added extra floors. Grandad and Hilda turned their spare room at the front of the bungalow into my bedroom. It had a nice view of the front garden. The back garden bordered a farmer's field where Christmas trees were grown for commercial sales. They played a lot of golf and Grandad liked to practise his tee-offing skills from his garden into that field. At the end of the glade, there was a field that had horses in it. Hilda sometimes went horse riding, and occasionally, we went up to the field to feed them. There was a forest behind the bungalows and at the end of the glade. These places became my new playground. Hilda had a fold-up bike with a back break which you could operate by pedalling backwards. I enjoyed taking Hilda's bike out with their dog, and we would ride up woodlands lanes. I had lots of time to play and explore here, because I didn't attend school whilst I was living at Grandad Charlie's.

When Grandad took me away from Mum and David, I was scruffy and unkempt. My clothes were tired and worn out and my socks were full of holes. Hilda took me to the local shops in Little Bookham at the first opportunity and bought me half a dozen pairs of new socks. That meant quite a lot to me, even at that age, because I cared a lot about my appearance and it felt good to know that someone else did too. In the evenings, we spent our time in the conservatory completing jigsaw puzzles together. Grandad owned a heating company. I was sometimes allowed to go with him when he visited sites to see how his employees were getting on. I loved tagging along and then going into the pie shop together on the way home to get a steak pie each. What I saw and experienced made such an impression on me that I wanted to be a heating engineer when I grew up.

One day during my stay at Grandad Charlie's, Hilda was sitting in the lounge. I had just walked in from the garden and she asked me to go into the dining room to get a book off of the table. I brought it back and sat down beside her. Hilda turned to the back of the book where there was a photograph of the author. It was the famous actor and film star, Steve McQueen. She pointed to the photograph and said to me, "That's you, Mark, you're a Steve McQueen lookalike." Hilda called me that every time I visited. It was a personal thing between me and her. Nobody else knew about it. On another occasion, Hilda pointed out a painting which had been hung on the wall in the hall opposite hers and Grandad's bedroom. The painting depicted an adult male sitting comfortably in a chair with a young girl stood close beside him. On the floor on the other side of the man, there was a red rotary dial telephone. Both of them looked happy. They were posing in a room with a large bay window behind them and the sunlight shone brightly through it.

Return to Tooting

I had been experiencing a relatively normal and happy life in Little Bookham, pretty much like I had done in the sixties at Nan Rose's flat. I felt 'at home' in Grandad and Hilda's company. Sadly, it was short-lived, and about eight months after Grandad rescued me from my living hell, he told me that it was time to go back. I didn't want to go back. Ever! But despite my obvious displeasure, I was made to return to Mum and David, who I now had to call dad. Life wasn't too bad at first. David left me alone for a while but, in time, he went back to his abusive ways. I tried my best to stay out of David's way and avoid doing things that might have gotten his attention. I enjoyed going swimming at Tooting Leisure Centre and often went there with my friends.

There was a joke shop on the way to the pool which we sometimes visited. On one occasion, we decided to go in there, and I bought a plastic flower. I thought that it would be a funny joke to play on someone because I could fill it with water, and when someone got near enough, I could squirt them with it. Earlier that day, David had given me ten pence to buy a bag of chips out of the chip shop that was opposite where we lived. I spent the money on the joke flower instead. My friend and I went back to my home after swimming and David was there. He asked, "Did you buy chips with me money that I gave to you, Mark?" I showed David the plastic flower and squirted it at him, but he didn't find it funny

I replied hesitantly, "No, I never got chips."

David then said to me, "Do you want six of the best in front of your friend or do you want them in your room?" I looked at David in shock and then to my friend who was standing awkwardly next to me. My friend's face dropped and he looked at the floor.

I chose to take them upstairs, thinking that my friend would be told to go home. But David told him to go into the front room and sit on a wooden chair. It was a room with high ceilings and the chair was in the middle. I was dragged by my arm upstairs and to my room where David made me drop my trousers and pants. All of the doors had been left open on purpose so that my friend who was sitting downstairs could hear what was going on. I was made to bend over and receive six very hard hits across my ass with a leather slipper. I didn't cry or make a single sound. Afterwards, I hurriedly pulled my clothes back up and we went downstairs where my friend was still sitting. He was then allowed to leave and went silently without speaking or giving any eye contact. I never invited my friends around again for fear of the same kind of humiliation.

It was now 1972. I was a new pupil at Hillbrook Primary School. I didn't get lifts or catch buses to school. I walked like everyone else. Looking back now, it was actually quite far. Mum and David got married that year and David changed my surname from Jennings to Graves. Not by deed poll – in those days, you could change a name as easily as choosing a new one and using it. I hated that surname, and I hated David. I wasn't to be known as a Jennings anymore, and I was not allowed to see anyone from the Jennings or Frohock family, except for Nan Rose and Grandad Charlie. But I didn't even see Nan as much as I had done previously.

I fell behind badly in my education after missing almost a year at school whilst I was with Grandad and Hilda. David blamed it on my eyesight rather than my absence. He and Mum thought that I was struggling to see the blackboard so Mum took me to have an eye test in Upper Tooting Road. The optician agreed that I needed to wear glasses to assist me with seeing the blackboard. I wore them in class, but I didn't like them. They had thick rims and wire arms that curled around my ears. One afternoon, I decided that I no longer wanted to wear my glasses so I went to the alleyway at the back of the houses and smashed them to pieces with a hammer. Nothing was ever mentioned about them. I don't think that anyone even noticed that my glasses had disappeared.

I was having to wear second-hand clothes and other people's cast-off shoes. When I went to Grandad's home for family dinners, his brothers were sometimes there too. They were always smartly dressed, wearing suits. Upon our arrival, Grandad would look me up and down and then turn to my mum saying, "Dress him better." But I reckon that he was mostly concerned about what his brothers would think and say. He didn't want to look bad in front of his family. I knew that I looked unkept and scruffy. Aunt Ciss must have thought that too. She gave me Uncle Ernie's gloves and scarves every now and then. They were the very best quality, and I felt privileged to have them. I looked after them with the utmost care. I didn't have very many decent pieces of clothing at that time, so I really appreciated being given these. My mental health was being impacted on. I had started to wet the bed.

In the road behind the alleyway, there was a church hall where Cubs and Scouts had their meetings. I eagerly joined the cubs group. It was a good way to get out of the flat and away from David. In 1973, the Cubs held a football match on Wandsworth Common. I was selected into the team and played centre. I scored two goals! I thought that I had played well and this made me feel really happy with myself. I went home that evening and played cards. We used to play cards quite often. Halfway through the card game, I started being sick. I vomited all over the table. I was rushed to hospital with a ruptured appendix and had an operation to have it removed. I stayed in hospital for a week. When I got discharged to go home, I was still suffering a lot of pain. After a week, the pain had not abated and there was a visible bulge in my abdomen where my appendix had been. I went back to the hospital where they opened my scar again whilst I was still awake. Foul smelling, green pus poured out like lava from a volcano. The wound had to be left wide open so that it could heal and close by itself, and I was ordered to have two salt baths a day to keep the wound clean. At home, I was walking around like a little old man with a walking stick, but it did heal up eventually, and I was allowed to return to school.

There was hardly ever any food in the flat. The only time that I was able to eat was when Mum cooked. Mum could not afford school dinners so she used to make sandwiches for my school lunches. But she didn't always have the food to do that so I sometimes had to go without. I returned home one day at lunchtime and discovered a couple of slices of bread in the kitchen. I put some brown sauce and vinegar on it and started to eat it just as David came in. He slapped me for eating what he called his food. It didn't matter to him that I would have gone hungry otherwise.

I hated David immensely! He had a big Coke bottle which he saved money in. From time to time, I took money out of the bottle, but only because I was hungry. David never noticed. Grandad and Hilda came over to visit us one evening. Grandad gave me fifty pence and told me to go and buy sweets with it. It was a lot of money in the seventies. I went straight to the shop and spent the lot on the biggest bar of chocolate that the shop had. I felt like Charlie out of *Charlie and the Chocolate Factory* – the part where Charlie finds the money and goes into the sweet shop to buy a large bar of chocolate. I savoured every single piece.

David spent his earnings in the pub. He was in there most nights drinking and would crawl back home completely hammered. Mum and I never knew what kind of mood he would be in when he returned home because he changed them like Jekyll and Hyde. If David came home drunk and Mum had made dinner for him, he would sometimes sit there, looking at his meal in disgust for a while before saying "What's this shit?" and throwing the plate up the wall. Mess was everywhere and Mum had no choice but to clean it all up.

Whenever David became very abusive to Mum, she never turned to her own family. She never asked for financial aid or emotional support. Instead, she would turn to David's family, especially his sister who was living in Stockwell at the time. Mum and I walked there, sometimes very late at night and stayed there for a couple of days or even a couple of weeks. David's sister was a good woman with a good heart. She refused to tolerate her brother's drunken behaviour and would insist that he go home. I couldn't understand why Mum kept going back to David.

Going to Leysdown

Mum and I didn't go abroad any more or stay at Grange Manor Farm. Instead, we went on holiday with David's family to Leysdown on the Isle of Sheppey. We stayed at one of the caravan parks in either a caravan or chalet. They were completely different holidays to the ones that I had experienced in the past, but they were still a lot of fun. Most of the kids came to the parks with their families from South London. It was a popular destination choice for Londoners due to its close location. In those days, all of the caravans and chalets were occupied and some of the parks laid on entertainment. One park in particular had an outdoor swimming pool with diving boards. It was a popular place to be and was always packed solid. Us kids had some great days in there. When the sea went out, we went cockling, which was great fun. We went to Leysdown a lot in the coming years. In fact, it was the only place we went that wasn't home. During the rest of the six-week holiday period, I was left at home alone whilst Mum and David were at work. I spent a lot of my time going fishing with one of the boys who lived not far from me. Sometimes, I would go out to ride my bike with two other boys from school.

Hillbrook School

By this time, I had missed a lot more schooling and my academic abilities fell even further behind those of my classmates. My reading and writing skills were not improving even though I was making a concerted effort. I now realise that I am dyslexic, but back then, kids with dyslexia were just labelled as thick. I got called that a lot. There was a lady teacher at school who held a small group of ten pupils or less. She helped us by using a technique of writing simple words that we used a lot onto cards. As we memorised those words, she introduced harder ones. I used to write a number of words on a card or in the back of my book so that I could refer back to them whenever I needed to. It helped me a lot because I didn't have to keep on asking people for assistance.

We played a lot of football at the school on the large playing fields which were next to the main building. There were some occasions when we were permitted to wear our own football kits to school. I had a Chelsea football kit with a number eight on the back of the shirt. It was bought for me when I lived with my mum at Nan Rose's flat. Us children were excitedly informed that Bobby Moore was making a special appearance at our school as part of the Bobby Moore Soccer for Schools programme. In the week preceding the visit, there was a lot of talk amongst the kids and the teachers. It wasn't every day that a celebrity came to visit us.

The day had arrived. Mum made sure the night before that my school clothes were clean and neatly ironed. Once in school, we got changed into our football kits before we were called into the playground and instructed to form a line. Bobby came to talk to us about the game, football and techniques of playing. It made me feel very excited to be able to see Bobby again. I was overwhelmed with joy. It had been a while since I had last been in Bobby's company, but I instantly recognised him. He was in the playground with another man who was also a professional football player. After the chat, we then went onto the school playing fields to practise and to be taught some ball control techniques. After I got changed back into my school uniform, I was invited to have a photograph taken with Bobby and his friend. I remember it to be a great day, and I enjoyed every moment of it immensely. I was a pupil at Hillbrook School until 1973. But sadly, I didn't finish that school year because we moved again.

Salcotte Road

We went to live in Salcotte Road, which was just off of Northcotte Road in Battersea. Our new place of residence was a flat in the basement of a house. It was only temporary accommodation as the local council were actively seeking us a permanent place to live. A young woman and her children lived in the other part of the house, and we all shared the garden. Down the end of the garden, there was an old shed. I was nine years old by that time, and the boy who lived above us was around the same age as me. We became very good friends. We spent many hours playing in the shared garden together. I loved to go to the cinema to watch films, and on a few occasions, we went together. We loved to watch action films like James Bond. James Bond was very popular in the sixties and seventies. And just like today, there were a lot of fans and followers. I was also friends with two girls that were the same age as me. Penny lived in the road opposite in a big townhouse and the other girl, Wendy, lived in Montholme Road, which was quite close to Honeywell School at the end of Northcote Road. We would go to each other's houses to play. Wendy wanted to be a drummer, and she was fortunate to have parents that were willing to invest in her dreams by buying her a full drum set. She had sisters too, but I can't remember their names now.

When I was nine, Nan's health began to worsen, and she was admitted to Westminster Hospital. When I went to visit her, I was met by quite a distressing sight. Nan was in a room alone with tubes in her arms and she was bringing up phlegm every five minutes. I found it so upsetting that I only saw her on a few occasions. One day, I was playing in the garden when a neighbour called me inside. I was told to go into the neighbour's home to receive a telephone call. Mum was ringing me from the hospital and she told me that Nan Rose had passed away. Because I was a child, I wasn't allowed to attend her funeral. She was buried at St Peter's Church in West Morely at St Paul's, which is also the church where other religious family events took place. My uncle, Lawrence Broad, was the pastor and carried out the Sunday Service at the same church. He was called Lorry by people who knew him well. He and Aunt Dolly are buried there along with other family members. Nan Rose's grave is next to the entrance wall. As a child, I missed her dearly, and I would continue to mourn her loss for the rest of my life. Aunt Ciss must have noticed this, and she fulfilled Nan Rose's role from then on. We would remain close for the rest of Aunt Ciss' life, which was a comfort and blessing to me because I was never very close to Mum for many different reasons.

Mum gave birth to a baby girl when we lived here. Mum and David called her Ann Graves. They were really happy to have a daughter. Once Ann was born, I had to share any money that I was given with her. But because Ann was only a baby, she never received any money because David used to keep it for himself. Mum used to get me to take Ann out with me. I even took her with me on the bus to David's sister's house in Stockwell. In her pram! Looking back, I can't believe that I did that at such a young age. Mum stopped working to become a housewife. David didn't want her to work anymore.

David had a niece who stayed with us from time to time. She was a couple of years older than me, but we got on with each other quite well. We had bunkbeds. I slept on the top bunk. Ann was still very young and slept in her cot next to Mum's bed. One night, Mum and David went out, and we both decided to climb out of bed and get up to some mischief. We were in for a right night of fun and games! It was dark outside, but it was coming towards the end of summer so it wasn't cold at all. It must have been sometime around eight o'clock when we went into the garden. The garden was flanked by other gardens on each side, and it had a high wall at the end. It spanned the length of all of the gardens. About ten gardens along from ours, we had noticed an apple tree and decided that that it would be great fun to give that garden a visit. We called it 'scrumping'. We both climbed up onto the wall and proceeded to walk gingerly along the top towards the garden with the tree. When we were about halfway along the wall, we both heard someone open their door and come outside so we jumped down into the garden to avoid been spotted. We noticed a child's playhouse so we quickly scampered inside to hide from the man who had stepped out of his door to investigate. We stayed as quiet and as still as we could. I remember feeling my heart beating so fast! We both watched for the man by peeping cautiously out of the playhouse windows. He didn't see us and eventually went back inside his house. We stayed hidden for a short while before we climbed back onto the wall and continued on towards the tree.

It's a wonder that we didn't get caught out by any other residents because we found it to be an amusing act and were laughing the whole time. We got to the apple tree, filled our pockets and a bag that we had brought with us, then returned along the wall to our own garden. Once back in the kitchen, David's niece decided that she would bake an apple pie. We knew that we were probably going too far at that point but must have just thought hi ho, here we go! She pulled the largest cooking pot out of the cupboard, placed it onto the gas cooker grill and filled it with apples until no more could fit in. We hadn't even peeled or sliced them! Just as she went to light the cooker, Mum and David returned home. Believe me when I say that David was not a happy bunny! His niece knew that she could do pretty much what she liked because David wouldn't have done anything to her that would have upset his sister. So I got his full rage. That was one time that it felt like it was worth getting though. I still laugh to myself every time that I think about that memory.

On the way home from Honeywell School, some of my friends and I liked to walk to a baker's shop that was on one of the street corners. The shopfront was painted brown and some of the delicious treats on offer were strategically displayed in the shop window to lure in passers-by. At the end of each day, any cakes that had not been sold were thrown out. The ladies behind the counter kindly put the leftover cakes in bags and sold them to us for 2p a go. Mum could not afford to buy me treats like cakes, or school dinners. I only ever took a packed lunch to school, which was sandwiches. I was often hungry so the cakes helped immensely. The same went for some of the other kids who also bought them.

We used to try to get free rides home on the back of the open buses too. We grabbed on to the long handle that ran down the length of the door. If the bus conductor saw us hanging on, we would jump off, even if the bus was moving. It was okay if we managed to jump off without incident. But if we rolled over into the road or onto the pavement, we ended up with cuts and grazes, especially on our legs. Lots of boys wore holes into their trousers. Our mums mended them with patches that were quite fun. They were unicorns or names, maybe a smiley face or NASA. You could literally get all kinds of patches. Years later, people would buy them to sew on and wear as part of fashion rather than to cover up a hole. When jeans became popular, girls and boys would put them on and get into the bath to shrink them to their body. They would also personalise them by putting them into a bucket of bleach and then heat them up on the stove. The jeans would go white, light blue and dark in colour giving them a pattern. Mods and Skinheads would often do this to their denim.

Tynham Close

Our next address was 14 Tynham Close in Shirley Grove. In those days, the council decorated homes before tenants moved in. I remember the first room on the right that was freshly painted with a small balcony looking over the communal garden. The bath and toilet were in two separate rooms next to each other and the next room on the left was the kitchen. It had a basic layout with a cooker, sink and a just few cupboards. We didn't have a washing machine. Mum and I took our washing to a launderette in Lavender Hill, near Queen's Town Road. The first bedroom was on the right side of the hallway, and then at the end, there were two more bedrooms with a door on opposite sides. Mum and David slept in the room on the right. But the flat had three bedrooms so I did get to have my own private space. The family that lived above us at our last address also moved a few weeks later to a new home in a street that wasn't very far away from us in Shirley Grove. I carried on being friends with the son for a few more years. Our mums became good friends too. It's a shame that I can't be sure of his name, but I have a feeling that it was Steve. A brand new estate was also built opposite our flats. When they were completed, lots of families moved in and I made a lot of new friends there. In fact, all of the kids in the roads around our area knew each other in one way or another.

In the autumn, us kids collected conkers from the horse chestnut trees. I sought out the biggest and best conkers that I could find and gleefully took them home with me. There was a tried and tested method for preparing conkers for battle. Firstly, I covered them in vinegar and soaked them for a couple of minutes, then they were baked in the oven on a low heat for a couple of hours to make them hard. Then the conkers were drilled right through the middle so that a string could be attached. The idea of the game was to break your opponent's conker. Players would take turns by holding their conker out in front of them and letting the opponent try to hit it with theirs. I liked to play this game outside with my friends and I also played it at school. Most kids also liked to play marbles. My friends and I collected marbles too. Everybody had one or two favourite marbles which were for showing off only, they seldom played with them. Unless they had their eye on someone else's and they found it hard to part with it. We took our marbles with us to school. The top of the drain cover in the playground with its parallel grooves used to be ideal for playing on. It was black and about 1 ft x 2 ft. But my most favourite pastime was building Airfix models. I started when I was seven years old and carried on making them up to the age of fifteen. I used to make detailed battlefield scenery out of papier mâché. I liked to construct a realistic scene with trees and mud, and then put Airfix tanks onto it just like a scene in World War II. I learned how to make those scenes in secondary school, but there were Airfix magazines available that showed people how to do it too. Us kids would sometimes play on the swings in the small playground at the bottom of the flats. I still liked to swim on a regular basis and would frequently go to Latchmere public swimming pool. I went with my school as part of my physical education, but I also liked to go there socially with my friends.

At the top of our road on the corner, there was a shop called Jay's which specialised in army surplus. They sold everything you could want from Dr Martins boots to army coats and trousers. You could also purchase tents and camping equipment from there. Next to that shop, there was a delicatessen where you could buy coffee, homemade bread, sliced meats, olives and a variety of cheeses. The first ever delicatessen had opened in Clerkenwell during the reign of Queen Victoria in 1878. It was called Terroni Deli and was in Lavender Hill. Customers could purchase specialities such as imported meats, cheeses and olives. There were pickled vegetables, dips and breads too. Customers were able to sit outside at two little tables and enjoy freshly made cups of coffee. It represented a new change in Battersea as an upcoming borough, and I believe that this was one of the first shops to offer this kind of outside table service. Next to the delicatessen, there was an off licence. They had a licence to sell alcohol that could be taken away and consumed off of the premises. They also sold fags. Mum and David smoked and they often sent me on errands to buy their fags, either from the newsagents or the off licence. The owners of both shops knew me and my family so they were happy to serve me because they were confident that I was buying them on their behalf. As well as running to and from the shop, Mum had me doing lots of jobs at home. After Mum had cooked, I would wash up. On Saturdays, it was my responsibility to polish the bits of furniture that needed it and to vacuum all of the carpets. These jobs had to be completed before I was allowed out with my friends.

Shirley Grove was not very far from Clapham Junction. Northcote Road had a market with many stalls selling fruit and vegetables. Clapham Junction had a vast variety of shops selling all kinds of goods. It was a place where many people would come to do their shopping, even if they had to travel from another area. It was a great place to shop. The biggest shop was Arding and Hobbs, and it was situated at the junction of Lavender Hill and St John's Road. It was a huge department store so you could buy all sorts of things there, from furniture to school uniform. I bought my first pair of rugby boots from there. There was lots of room to display all of the goods on offer, and it was very well laid out.

Being with Steven

David had a younger brother called Steven Graves. He was nothing like the rest of his family. Maybe it was because he had been adopted. When I met Steven, he was quite young, late teens to early twenties maybe. We became very good friends and spent a great deal of time in each other's company. He had a passion for football, and his favourite team was Chelsea, who played at Stamford Bridge. He went to all of Chelsea's home games and most of their away games too. Steve played football at the weekends at Blackheath Or Clapham Common. He took me with him and we would go in all weather conditions. We didn't care about getting wet or being blown by strong winds, especially on the heath. We hadn't known each other for long before Steve started taking me to the matches. He always paid for me to go and collected Chelsea match programmes. They were carefully stored in a folder in their own plastic wallets. Steve made one for me too.

I didn't really like football, but when we went to see Chelsea play, I loved the roar of the crowds! When a goal was scored, the cheers resonated loudly around the stadium. I revelled in the highs and the lows, the anticipation and the suspense, the thrill of the win and the disappointment of the losing side. Watching the game live was totally different to watching it on the telly. When I went to watch Chelsea Peter Bonetti was in goal, and at that time, he was at the top of his game. For some reason, I felt a strong connection, but I didn't know why. A couple of seasons later, Steve and I stopped going to watch Chelsea and started going to Wimbledon Football Club. Their home turf was at Plough Lane and the team had just been promoted to the fourth division. Over the space of four years, we watched them go from fourth to first division. It was the best football that I ever saw.

When Steve got into a relationship with a woman called Janet, they both moved into a flat on the top floor of a house in Balham. It was opposite Tooting Bec Common and just off of Emanuel Road. I started to favour weekends with Steven and Janet over those spent with Grandad Charlie. Janet always cooked great meals. One that we had quite often was sausages, mash and peas. For a laugh, Steve would eat half of one of my sausages and push the eaten end into the mash to disguise it. It happened so often that I knew what the outcome would be, but we would still laugh really hard every time I discovered the half-eaten sausage. Steven was always busy doing something.

Steven had lots of different hobbies. We tried golf for a short while, and then we did mud larking on the Thames foreshore. One evening, I remember being at Steven's when he asked me if I would like to go mud larking with him. I agreed straightaway. We drove in the dark from Balham to Westminster. We took torches with us so that we could see where we were searching on the foreshore. I was very excited even though I did not know what to expect as I had never heard of mud larking before. Everything that I did with Steven was good fun. We drove across Westminster Bridge to the opposite side of the river, facing St Thomas' Hospital. Steven parked the car on Lambeth Palace Road, and we went on to the foreshore via a set of stone steps.

The mud was soft, and I could feel my feet sinking into it. I hurriedly tucked my trousers into my socks in an attempt to keep them clean. Neither of us had wellington boots, and I was about to learn that mistake the hard way. The moon, bright lights on the bridge and the lights on passing river boats cut through the darkness and cast shadows onto the riverside. As we walked towards the river, I noticed the shape of a man bending down in the water. He was holding something with both hands. As we got nearer, I could see that it was an old potato sieve. The man was dipping it in and out of the water.

The man also had an old wheelbarrow near to him and a spade. I went up to him and asked him what he was doing. He explained that he was digging up clumps, then using the sieve to wash the mud away to reveal anything that might have been buried in it. He asked me if I would like to have a go and I gleefully accepted his offer. He showed me how to do it and helped me to look through the mud. I soaked my feet, but I didn't care. It was great fun. The man then showed me some of the things that he had discovered and I was fascinated by his horde.

After that first time, I was bitten by the bug and could not wait to go mud larking again. I had a good eye for finding things when we were together on the banks. I liked to collect clay tobacco pipes that had been discarded by dockers and other ship and boat workers. I amassed a considerable collection, with pipes in many designs ranging from the sixteenth century onwards. I also found quite a lot of ammunition. I liked to take bullets home and clean them up with an emery cloth, which was really quite dangerous because they were still live. With a bit of attention, they would come up very well, just like new. I also collected old bottles in all different shapes and sizes.

When we had first started going to the foreshore together, Steven found a Colt .45 handgun. It was obvious to see that it had been there for a long time as it was encrusted in mud that had become quite hard. Steven still took it though. He had it acid dipped to sadly discover that half of the handle was missing and that it could not be used any more. I think that it probably would have been a good showpiece, but not long after that, Steven and I went down to the Thames, and he threw it back into the water. He never gave me a reason why he chose to do that. Steven and I returned to the same spot several times, and I saw the man there a few times, too.

Honeywell School

I still had to walk to Honeywell School from our new home, and it was a much longer journey. One day, I met up with a few school friends who lived off of Lavender Hill. We all walked along to the end of Webb's Road to a small courtyard where we discovered some old window frames that still had the glass panes in them. They had been left on the ground leaning up against a wall. I picked up an old broomstick that had been left lying around and put the end of it through one of the windows. I didn't anticipate that the pane would break so easily and the broomstick went through it really fast, so fast that my hand went through it too. I had a cut on the side of my palm about an inch long and the same in depth. I pulled a handkerchief from my pocket and wrapped it around my hand to stop the bleeding. When I got home, I applied two plasters in a butterfly shape to keep the wound closed. I didn't tell Mum. The scar still shows today to remind me how stupid we were, because it wasn't only me who broke windows.

The other kids made fun of me because of how behind I was from the rest of the class. I had many playground fights too with other kids who decided to pick on me. I won them all! One boy had to have stitches in his mouth after picking a fight with me. I kicked him in the face when he tried to get up from the ground. There was a group of girls who used to go around in a group bullying and picking on me. When they were together, they acted very spitefully, and it was quite overwhelming to have to put up with it day after day. Eventually, I snapped. My classroom was one of two portable cabins that were situated at the end of the playground. I took the biggest girl around the back and hit her straight in the stomach! I told her that if the bullying carried on, I would take them one at a time and do the same thing. From then on, they left me alone. I finished my primary education at Honeywell Primary, but I didn't do the 11+ exam.

One evening, I'd been playing out with my friends until dark, when I came home to see a gleaming red Jag parked right outside the flats. I went up the stairs to our flat and went inside. I walked into the front room and saw Mum sitting in an armchair that was facing the doorway. There was also another person, a blonde man, sitting in the small sofa next to her. He had his back to me. He didn't turn to acknowledge my presence or speak whilst I was there. I do remember that he was wearing a suit and that he sat very straight with broad, muscular shoulders. I put two and two together and assumed that the Jag outside must have belonged to him. I cannot remember what Mum said to me that evening, but I didn't stay in the room for very long. I was astonished that Mum had a male stranger in the flat while David was not home. Mum never invited men over. It made me wonder who the strange man could be and why he was sitting in our flat?

William Blake

The summer holidays were coming to an end, and it was almost time to start my secondary school education. There didn't appear to be any choice about where I would go because I had been so far behind in my learning compared to my peers. Mum told me that she could only get me into the school in Bridge Lane, Battersea. It was called William Blake Comprehensive School forBoys.

I don't know if she ever applied to any of the other schools in the borough of Lambeth. New school uniform was quite expensive. Mum couldn't afford it so she had to apply for school clothes vouchers. We were expected to wear a smart uniform that consisted of a black blazer, white shirt, grey trousers, school tie and black shoes. I had brown shoes that I managed, after some effort, to change colour with black shoe polish. We had to have the school badge on the pocket of the blazer. Mum bought mine without the badge and I sewed it on myself.

On my first day at the new school, I got up at seven o'clock and started my routine by washing my face and brushing my teeth. I then had my breakfast, which was Weetabix more often than not. If there was no milk, I would boil some water and pour that over them. I cleaned and polished my shoes before getting dressed. If I saw creases in my uniform when I took it from the cupboard, I ironed them all out. I took a deep pride in the way that I looked and always presented myself in the best way possible. My school jumper had not been bought in a shop. Aunt Ciss lovingly handknitted one for me instead. She was good like that. I remember how proud I felt wearing my new school uniform. My mother never came to my school, I walked there unaccompanied. In the seventies, that's what we did. Apart from the fact that it was in Battersea, somewhere I'm not certain that she knew where it was. My friends and I knew the streets very well so I knew the way that I had to walk to get there. Most of the boys lived in Battersea, and we always met up along the way. I walked along the back roads and across a railway foot crossing towards Latchmere

Road before turning down towards Bridge Lane. I remember feeling very nervous as I did not know what to expect when I arrived at school.

I entered the school gates for the very first time and walked straight into the main playground. To the right of the playground, there was a brick shelter with supporting metal beams running from the back wall to the front of the gable roof. A fixed bench ran along the entirety of the back wall. When I arrived, there were only three or four of us in the playground because it was still early and school didn't start until nine o'clock. The main school building could be seen through the railings that ran along the road and it could be accessed from the left side of the playground. Going further into the grounds, past the main building, there was a smaller building that had labs in them for physics and chemistry lessons. This was on the right side and it was the same height as the main building. Further on, there was another playground. Looking to the main building, part of it stuck out. The gymnasium was on the ground floor and the main hall was directly above it. When it was nine o'clock, all of the first year boys were herded into the main hall. We were separated into three classes. I was put into class three, which I soon learned was the class for boys who were behind or had learning difficulties. The kitchen area could be found at the furthest end of the ground floor. That's where we had to queue up for lunches. A few of us would go back for seconds, which the dinner ladies would give to us willingly.

I was put into class three because I needed support with my reading, writing and my mathematics. It was like starting school all over again. I was shown how to write words as well as letters and my maths was coming along nicely. Looking back, I realised that there were three or four other boys that had the capability to excel and should have been in a higher class. We got to know each other well in the following months. I had been at the school for about six months when a maths competition was held in the main hall. A stage was specially set up at the window end of the hall. Chairs had been set out in neat rows. The students and teachers filed in through big, double doors that were at each end of the hall to sit down in teams. Three boys had been selected from each class, and we proudly took our place on the stage. A teacher asked maths questions to each of the teams. I got a lot of our team's questions right, but it wasn't enough to win on that occasion. I had done well though, and my efforts were noticed by several teachers, including the one who had organised the competition. A couple of weeks later, I was moved out of class three and promoted to class two. I did much better there as there were boys at my level as well as above me, especially in English classes.

Battersea Park was in close proximity to the school so we went there to play cricket. I found that I was good at the game, and in later years, I would become a very good bowler. The school organised for students to visit the Oval Cricket Ground to watch a few matches. I found them absolutely boring due to the sport being very slow and laid back. It wasn't for me, even though I was picked for the school team a few times. William Blake was known as a football school, and there were others who specialised in either football or rugby. My school had quite a good football team whilst I was studying there. The curriculum offered a wide variety of sports. I took up canoeing, badminton, basketball, fixed-wheel cycle racing, gymnastics and cricket.

I now ask myself how we managed to do all of these sports activities. Cricket was only played in the summer months after the football season had finished. We went canoeing all year around at Ham Dock in Surrey. Believe me when I say that it was very cold in the winter months! We played hi ball, where you had to throw a ball at the other team to get them out. Someone always ended up capsizing into the water. There was very little time to get out and then back into the canoe. There was a way that it had to be done. Two other canoeists would come to steady the upturned canoe from each side with their paddles so that the boy could help himself up and in. If you got it wrong, you could become unwell very quickly from the cold of the water. There weren't any health and safety regulations in those days. As we became stronger and more confident, we were allowed to canoe down and back up again on the Thames. Depending on which way the tide was coming, one way was harder to navigate than the other. Paddling against the tide was very tiring.

We went to Crystal Palace to take part in cycle racing on a cycle racing track which was part of the Olympic venue. The cycles had a fixed wheel and no breaks, meaning that they had to be slowed down by using the pedals. We trained on rollers, which was quite scary as the track was only about a foot wide and we were expected to train in a very small room. If anyone was unfortunate and came off, they would really hurt themselves. But it was great to take part and compete against other boys in my class and the rest of the school. In the winter months, it was extremely cold. We used roughed-up newspaper to keep our legs warm by stuffing it into our trousers. We wore blue plastic helmets to protect our heads on the track. I always enjoyed cycling, whether it was on the track or with my friends on the road.

When we had P.E. in the gym, we could climb the ropes and touch the ceiling with our hands. At first, I found it very hard to climb up the rope as my muscles were not strong enough to climb up to the top. But after months of hard work building up those muscles, I did achieve it. I wasn't the kind of boy who would give up on something after the first try. I would always have a go. There was vaulting bench that we were taught different ways of getting over. A couple of the boys were really agile and were able to perform backflips. I never attempted to try that; it looked too dangerous so I left that one. But fair play to the boys that could. It made other boys, including myself, very envious. During the dinner period, boys were invited to attend gymnastics classes and I took part in them. There was a climbing apparatus which was pulled away from the wall. It was tall, almost to the ceiling, with metal bars for climbing up on. We didn't have badminton courts on the school grounds so we went York Road. They were used by the local schools in the area. We played doubles or singles. I preferred doubles, but it was all good fun.

I never took up football as a main interest and I was never picked to play in any school teams. There were too many boys that wanted to play. It was like a closed group, and to me, it wasn't worth trying. I watched a lot of rugby on the TV, especially the international games, and this was the sport that I was more drawn to. I sometimes played football in the school playground but not much more than that. Other times, I would sit with my friends on the benches that were around the two playgrounds. There were some lunchtimes where I went with a group of boys over to Battersea Park and play. An adventure playground had recently been built, which had an entrance near to our school. Because of this, a lot of boys would go over there. In comparisons to today's play areas, it was quite dangerous. It was all made from recycled wood, which was sometimes painted in bright colours. There was a go-kart, also constructed from wood, at the top of a sloping platform which went right down to the ground. The go-kart would travel down the slope at quite a speed. Kids would often fall off and graze their knees and elbows, making holes in their clothes which didn't go down well with the parents.

I enjoyed lessons in the woodwork shop, cutting wood, shaping it and making something out of it. Something useful like a stool or a tray that I could take home afterwards. The first time that I received a punishment from the teacher I was in and art class on the top floor of the main building. I recall that I was laughing about something. The female teacher ordered me to hold out my hand and open it, palm upwards. I did as I was told and, before I knew it, she slapped my hand hard with a ruler. It bloody hurt! Apart from that, I enjoyed art classes, especially pottery and drawing.

Boys bullied other boys frequently whilst in school. I think that every school had a certain amount of bullying going on and I'm sure that it still goes on today. I didn't like to be bullied, or to witness another boy being a victim. I had had enough of that at Honeywell School. I never told anyone at William Blake about all of the fighting that I had gotten into. Anyone who tried to bully me had a shock when they attempted to bully me. Some boys would just take a disliking to someone. One boy in particular used to constantly stare at me with a screwed up face. One day, I was walking with one of my friends down from one floor to the floor below. The stairs were concrete with solid hard brick walls next to them. This boy was walking up the stairs to the left, and when he was about two steps away from me, he looked directly into my face. I had had enough of his attempts at intimidating me so I grabbed his head by his hair with my left hand and slammed it into the wall. I immediately saw that a big lump had appeared and he looked dazed. I don't think that he knew where he was.

My friend and I left the boy where he was and continued to walk downstairs. Nobody ever knew what had happened in the stairwell. If there was a fight, it was usually in the playground. Students who fought on the school grounds were certain to get a detention. Boys were expected to stay after normal school hours had finished for an extra hour. If the misdemeanour was serious, detentions would be every day for a week. Boys were rarely expelled, or sent home. I think that the teachers knew that if a boy was sent home, they would receive an even harder punishment. I never took a day off of school because school life was better than home life. If I had enough money, I liked to buy a packet of biscuits to take to school. My favourite choices were custard creams or bourbon creams. On one particular occasion, it was playtime, but I had decided to go back to my classroom on the first floor. Two older boys followed me into the school building from the playground and up the stairs. There were two classrooms that faced each other at the end of each corridor. When the boys caught up with me, they pushed me into the doorway of one of the classrooms. They leant menacingly over me, but they weren't very much taller. They ordered me to turn out my pockets, and I refused to do it. I told them that I didn't like bullies, and they began to push me hard against the door. As the left one came closer with his face, I hit him hard. I hit his nose with so much force that it broke and blood burst out everywhere. The boy was shocked as he hadn't expected it. His mate looked at him and they then turned to me and steamed into me together. I was already in a corner and I put both of my arms up to shield my face so that they couldn't get at me. Of course, it didn't stop them from trying though! We were all marched to the headmaster's office. The boys both got a good telling off, and I had to sit in the headmaster's office for the rest of the day. Those boys never touched me again and always greeted me with a kind manner from then on. I think that I had earned some kind of respect for not showing them any fear and standing my ground. I doubt that they had ever experienced that before.

Playing with Friends

After school, I enjoyed playing outside on my purple Chopper. I liked my bike, but I had always wanted the original red one. I took it everywhere with me, out to play locally or ride it to Stockwell to see my friends and then ride home. It looked like a good bike, but it wasn't very good to drive. It had trouble getting into gear properly and then the chain would come off or a link would snap. I was always fixing it.

In the summer months, my friends and I hired boats out on the boating lake at Battersea Park. It was pretty good fun. We didn't roll our boat around a lot because some of us would end up in the lake. Of course, we all splashed each and ended up soaking wet, especially if there were quite a few of us and we had more than one boat to share. We were only allowed to keep the boats out for an allotted time before we had to return them. We often went overtime and took ourselves to the other end of the lake, out of sight of the hut, so that the man who looked after the boats could not see us. They were supposed to be moored up and stored beside the hut. But we didn't return them to avoid paying the extra money.

The lake was not very deep so we could stand in it. The entrance and exit were also beside the hut so we had to be careful not to be seen when we left without returning our boat. Next to the lake on the far side, there is a set of large, different sized rocks that we used to like climbing onto and then jumping across from one rock to another. Over the years, the council made the park safer and installed metal fencing around the stones to stop children from climbing onto them, most likely due to new health and safety regulations. The park was a popular place for families to come and enjoy their leisure time. My friends and I would go frequently to sit around the pond in the park. A couple of them liked to have a go at catching the fish with rods.

Right beside the lake, there was a restaurant. It is still there to this day and is now called the Pear Tree Cafe. It used to have glass panels in white, metal frames and French doors that went in a semi-circle shape overlooking the lake. The dining tables were white and made of metal. It was a great place for people to visit, and it was always packed with people. A popular refreshment choice was a cup of tea and a slice of cake. Us boys bought stink bombs from small toy shops or joke shops. They came in little sealed, glass bottles that had the capability to clear a room when the top broke off or was smashed on the floor. They had an awful smell, absolutely nasty. As boys, we couldn't help ourselves. If we saw a lot of people sitting in the restaurant, we would break one, or even two at a time and watch the ensuing commotion unfold. For best effect, we always made sure that we closed the doors behind us. We thought that it was hilarious, but the people stuck with the stench inside never did. We let the stink bombs off in class at school too. That was quite amusing as the teacher never found out who the culprit was. We never told on each other.

Clapham Common was not very far from where I lived. Sometimes, my friends and I would go to play in a playground situated on the south side of the common. One of the main draws was a massive slide. When I was at the top of it, I felt so high up. It meant that the descent was very fast. So fast that I sometimes sped off of the end onto the concrete slab on the ground. Kids ended up grazing their knees or their elbows. Parks then were a far cry from today's with their spongy, black mats, and the slides are nowhere near as tall any more. I loved to play on the swings, and as I built up my confidence, I stood up on the seat and swung as high as I possibly could. It made me feel as if I was flying in the sky. There were see-saws that were pretty much wooden planks that often hit the asphalt directly. They gave us kids wood splinters, pinched fingers and spinal injuries. We liked to play on the Spinmee roundabout. Some of the older boys and girls liked to grab the handlebars which went from the middle of the roundabout to the outside, then run to make it go faster and faster, until they couldn't hold on any more. The other kids, who were usually smaller, sat on the top whilst holding onto the bars so that they didn't fall off. Another game that we played was 'drop off and pick up', where one kid let go of an object whilst on the spinning roundabout and then the others attempted to retrieve it. There were climbing frames that my friends and I liked to hang off of and use our hands to move from one bar to the next. They were also known as monkey bars.

Back at School

During the second year at William Blake, I proved to be a quick learner and started to do well in all of my subjects. I was making really good efforts at catching up with my schooling. I had grown considerably over the last year and my school uniform was getting too small for me. I was unable to lift my arms fully whilst wearing my shirt without tearing it. I kept asking Mum for new shirts. I often had to stitch up the crotch of my trousers too. I became quite adept at repairing my clothes with a needle and some cotton. One morning, I noticed really badly that my shirts needed to be replaced. The buttons looked as if they wanted to pop open! Mum came into the bedroom, and I commented to her that I was now in desperate need of some bigger shirts. But she just looked and said that they were all right. So I lifted my arms above my head and the shirt literally ripped open. I didn't need to say a word and nor did she. I got my shirts. When I walked to school in the morning, I went with friends that I met along the way. Most of the boys that walked with me went to Sinjun's and William Blake. We shared the same route as both schools were quite close together. To me, Sinjun's was by far the best school in Battersea, and I often told my mother that my wish was to be a student there.

It was standard practice to use a fountain pen with a nib in class. It was the type of pen that had to be dipped in liquid ink that was drawn from a reservoir. The ink came in a jar with a screwed lid. When people talk about pen or ink fights, this is the pen that they are talking about. In class, we often removed our blazers and hung them on the backs of our chairs. Boys sitting behind found it funny to flick ink all over the back of the boy in front's shirt. Sometimes, the victims wouldn't even know that they had done it.

The year 1976 was the hottest British summer that had ever been recorded. This meant that the River Thames was at its lowest level and I was able to go onto parts of the foreshore that were unreachable under normal circumstances. Steve and I went to the river a lot that summer. We also met up with a couple of other people who liked to mud lark and knew the best spots for finding. This particular day was very hot, and we had walked quite a long way along the embankment. We moved in a westerly direction next to Westminster Bridge, then towards Lambeth Bridge and on to Vauxhall Bridge.

A man joined us on the walk that day. When he started to talk, I realised that he was the same man that we had met on our night mud larks at Westminster. He was chatty and talked constantly, mostly to me, but he kept a distance of about two metres. The man was always smiling and often had a cheeky grin on his face. And he made me laugh! He was easy to talk to, like we already knew each other. But he did look a bit out of place due to what he was wearing. His trousers were very baggy, he wore a coat and had a hat on his head. Very overdressed for the weather that we were experiencing. He also had an old, metal wheelbarrow that he pushed along the embankment. I just assumed that he had found it down there somewhere. Despite his odd appearance, he was a pleasant man. Steve and I saw him a few more times that summer. The last time was when we walked between Chelsea Bridge and Albert Bridge. We never saw him again after that.

Jubilee Day

It was 7 June 1977. Her Majesty was fifty-one years of age and the nation was celebrating the twenty-fifth anniversary of her accession to the British throne and other Commonwealth realms. Millions took to the streets to celebrate our queen's Silver Jubilee and crowded into the mall in Central London. Most of the streets apart from the main roads were closed so that people could party with their relatives, friends and neighbours. Tables were taken out of people's homes and carried into the street to form one longer table, covered in white paper tablecloths, then laid with paper cups and plates. Some tablecloths were made to look fancy with patterns carefully cut out of them. There were many offerings brought to the tables such as cakes, sandwiches, fruit squash and water. Each kid was given a party hat to wear, and we all had Union Jack flags on sticks to wave around. Strings of bunting were hung across the streets in a zigzag fashion between windows and lampposts. Residents even brought out their sound systems so that everyone could enjoy their favourite hits of the time.

I remember it to be a very hot and sunny day. Many of us were wearing shorts and T-shirts. The street party that I attended was on the new estate across the road from my flat. It was around midday when everyone began to congregate. One of my friends approached me and said that my mum wanted me to go home straightaway to see her so I rushed back. When I got home, David was there, and he told me to go to the shop to get him a packet of cigarettes. He gave me the money, and I left right away. The roads were empty at this time. I walked to the top of the road, then a little bit along Lavender Hill until I faced the newsagent which was on the opposite side of the road. I didn't look as I took a step out into the road.

The next thing that I knew I was in St George's hospital. I had been hit by a red car. I didn't remember anything else. A witness said that the car had been going at some speed when it hit me. I had put my hands out to try to stop the car and then it knocked me up into the air. I ended up with a terrible cut to my forehead and other parts of my head were very bruised. I also had bruises over my body, but other than that, I was okay. It was a miracle that there weren't any breakages or lasting damage. I was lucky to be alive really! As a precautionary measure, I was made to remain in hospital for about a fortnight. During my stay, Mum had come to visit me with my little sister, Ann. But it wasn't until I was discharged and allowed to go home that I saw David.

David came alone to pick me up, and almost straightaway, he asked me what had happened to the money that he had given me for the cigarettes. I had to tell him that I lost it because it was in my hand at the time of the accident. It was plainly obvious that he then had the hump. He hadn't asked me anything like 'How are you?', 'Have you been okay?'. No, he just asked about the money. I asked David if he had brought any clean clothes for me to wear home. The ones I arrived in were bloodstained from the accident. He replied, "No, you'll have to go home in your pyjamas." He then asked me again in a stern voice about the whereabouts of the money he had given me. But I really didn't have a clue. It had probably been left on the road after I was picked up. Either someone else picked it up, or it was just left there. We had to ride a couple of buses to get home. I felt embarrassed walking about in my pyjamas. David must have wanted me to feel that way, otherwise he would have brought me some other clothes to wear home instead. It was as if he actually had the hump with me for getting run over, like it was a proper inconvenience. He was void of any kind of care or compassion. You could say no change there then!

Time with Steven

Steve and Janet had an old family dog. His name was Sheppey and he was half Alsatian, half Border Collie. I would take Sheppey for walks around the field of a park near to their home. Steven then went on to get another dog which they called Joe. He was also a mongrel and half the size of Sheppey. Both dogs got on together, and they were really well behaved. When I stayed overnight, I slept in the front room and the dogs would sleep next to me. I was allowed to watch telly until I fell asleep. I liked to watch football and would normally be asleep quite quickly. Steven did driving jobs, so at weekends and during the school holidays, I would like to stay over and go out with him to work. We even took the dogs with us.

One of the jobs that he did was for Freeman's catalogue. Customers typically bought stuff like clothes, shoes, furniture and bikes. At the time, it was a popular company because customers could spread their payments out over weeks, or even months. For many people, it was the only way that they could afford to purchase these items. I used to go with Steven on his round. At the start of the day, he would first get out an A–Z map book and mark out all of the stops that we needed to make. I took the customer's parcels to their front doors, and by the end of the round, I had done quite a lot of footwork. Steven rewarded my work with two pounds on Saturdays, but he saved up for me rather than give it to me.

Steven knew what Mum was like for money and that she would take every penny that she could get her hands on. Steven saved my earnings so that I had some spending money for a two-week holiday that he and Janet had booked. We were due to go in the school holidays. When it was about a week before my time to go on holiday with Steven and Janet, Mum took a couple of buses from where we lived in Battersea to Balham and demanded the money that Steven had put aside for me. It wasn't a lot; roughly ten or twelve pounds at the most. But Mum must have gone out of her way to collect it because she needed it to put meals on the table. David was working as a labourer on a building site, but he didn't earn a reliable income because sometimes he didn't bother turning up. I still went on the holiday to Eastbourne with Steven and Janet, even though I did not have any spending money. It was a very popular King's Holiday Camp, with chalets and a large clubhouse which had entertainment on two levels. Upstairs, there was a huge dance floor for guests to enjoy and the management would hire some really good groups to perform live music onstage. At the rear of the clubhouse, there was an outdoor swimming pool.

The concept was pretty much the same as the Butlins holiday camps. I never, ever asked Steven for any money, but he did give me some money when I needed it. On the second week of our holiday, I was listening to the radio in the chalet alone while Steven and Janet enjoyed the entertainments in the clubhouse. I can vividly recall the broadcaster announcing the unexpected death of Elvis Presley. It was the evening of 16 August 1977. The actual cause of death was a heart attack and the broadcaster said that Elvis had been found face-down on the floor of his spacious bathroom. He was the King of Rock and Roll. An absolute legend. When Steve came back to the chalet with Janet, I told them the sad news, but Steve didn't believe that Elvis was dead until it was announced again and he heard it for himself. I think that Steve was quite a fan back in the day. Despite the sad news about Elvis, it was still a great holiday and I loved every minute of it. The entertainments team held tournaments to keep holidaymakers busy throughout the day. I entered draughts and chess competitions. I won the draughts competition and came third in the chess tournament. I was gutted about the chess one as I thought of myself as quite a good player. In the following years, I seldom lost a draughts match and I improved my chess talent, too.

My school reports were getting a lot better and my grades were improving at the same time. My teachers left comments for each subject, including my maths teacher who commented about my personality. "Mark has a very dry sense of humour." It's nice to know that he saw me as clever and entertaining at the same time. Over time, I had become very settled in my schoolwork, and I no longer had to worry about threats or intimidation from bullies. I was left alone, apart from a few boys who wanted to have fights with me. I stayed away from fighting situations if I could, but there were occasions where someone would manage to push me to my limits. They ended up wishing that they had never bothered. I had good success in practical subjects such as woodwork, metal work and art.

I enjoyed drawing with a pencil onto paper and became quite skilled at shading in to give a picture depth. One of our neighbours had a teenage daughter who was very talented at painting with oils. She displayed some of her creations proudly on the walls in their flat. She helped me to do a few oil paintings of my own and gave me some of her educational art books, which helped me to improve my own drawing techniques. My paintings weren't bad at all, and I even sold some to Mum's friends. I mostly enjoyed painting during the summer months. In winter, I liked to build my Airfix models. I would continue to paint for the next two years.

The Merger

A month had passed since I had engaged in the conversation with Mum about how much I wanted to be a Sinjun boy. I met up with my Sinjun friends as usual to walk to school. One of the boys told me that Sinjun's and William Blake were to combine into one school as of September 1978. I felt like the luckiest kid alive in that moment and couldn't quite believe what I had just heard. My wish was coming true! Sinjun's was to be downgraded from a boy's grammar school to a comprehensive. It displeased a lot of people; teachers, pupils and parents at the school, as well as those who were connected to Sir Walter Saint John's School. William Blake was to become the lower school with Sinjun's becoming the upper school. I regarded Sinjun's as being one of the most prestigious secondary schools in Battersea, apart from Emmanuel School, which was independent and well known for pupils playing rugby throughout their time in education there. It was a boy's school at the time, and I knew a couple of them as one of my friends that went to Sinjun's had a brother who went there. Most of the teachers that had been employed at Sinjun's stayed on. Only a few left before the merge. I needed new clothes items for school as the uniform list for Sinjun's was quite extensive. I needed a new tie and a school badge for my blazer, a pair of white shorts, top and a pair of plimsolls for P.E. and a red shirt for rugby. I then had the task of removing the William Blake badge from my blazer and replacing it with a Sinjun's badge. I remember the feeling of pride when I wore my uniform. I felt good about the identity that it gave me. Sinjun's was about to change my life in a good way and assist me with my education immensely.

Sir Walter Saint John School is in Battersea, along the high street. It is close to William Blake School and not very far from the River Thames. The way that the school looked at the front reminded me of an old church. It had black railings that went the full length of the school and were about five feet high. Behind the railings, there was a green hedge with a neatly maintained gable cut top. At the entrance, there was an inscription that said, 'Rather Deathe Than False of Faythe'. Directly above it, there was the school's coat of arms. Some of the windows had stained-glass arches. The entrance to the school had two glass panels and was right in the middle of the front building. The entrance doors were large and heavy. The teachers had a separate car entrance to the pupils which could be found on the far right. Opposite the entrance to the school, there was couple of blocks of flats.

I woke at the crack of dawn for my first day at Sinjun's and got ready. I had cereal for breakfast, got dressed into my new school uniform. I walked to the house of a friend who lived by. Thomas was a Sinjun's pupil too, and I often played chess with him and some other boys that met at his house. When I got there, Thomas had set up a match to play before we left. After that, we walked to school through the back roads and towards Latchmere Road. We passed quite close to the lower school as we made our way to the upper school. As I glanced in the direction of the old William Blake building, I had no regrets and knew deep down that my life was about to get a lot better. My friends and I were all together at the same school. We were greeted and inspected by Mr Taylor, the school principal, when we reached the main entrance. The boys and teachers alike had a lot of respect for Mr Taylor, and I found him to be pretty fair. He had a good character.

The head prefect was called Richard. Both Mr Taylor and Richard wore black robes that day. Richard placed the greatest importance on his personal appearance. He always made sure that he was well groomed with his neatly pressed shirt tucked into his trousers, highly polished shoes and a straight tie. As we came into school, Richard would always be there with Mr Taylor scrutinising our appearances. Our shoes had to be black. If we got caught wearing trainers, we got sent straight home again. Anyone with an untucked shirt was made to tuck it in and ties had to be straight! Boys from different schools had started a trend of wearing ties very short whilst keeping the knot loose to make them wider and leaving the top button of their shirt undone. I never liked that style. Mr Taylor would make boys who flouted the rules remove their ties, tuck their shirts into their trousers and put their ties on correctly. He said that when boys were in the school or representing the school, they had to dress smartly and act in a responsible manner. I never got pulled up for that particular misdemeanour. I preferred to wear my tie the correct way with the top button of my shirt neatly fastened. But there were times when my shirts became too tight and I had no choice but to leave the collar loose. Nobody noticed because I concealed it with my tie.

Assembly was carried out in the big hall. It started with the singing of hymns and a welcome to all of the new Sinjun boys. Mr Taylor walked down the middle of the hall from the back, between the boys who were sitting on each side. He had Blakey's protectors in the heels of his shoes that made a distinct sound on the wooden floor. It didn't take me long to be able to tell when Mr Taylor was approaching by hearing alone. Mr Taylor walked up onto the stage. The principal and also Mr JJ O'Brien. The teachers flanked the hall on each side and stood at the back, too. There were steps on each side of the stage with a black piano to the left. There were seats for about six people on the stage to sit on during the assembly. They would take it in turns to speak to the rest of the school. Mr JJ O'Brian was head of both the lower and upper schools from 1977 to 1985.

The school's discipline was a lot stronger and more harsh than what I had experienced at William Blake. Pupils were disciplined more frequently with the cane. Richard had prefects who acted out beneath him. They were senior pupils who were authorised to enforce discipline on the rest of the pupils by the headmaster. For some reason, Richard took an instant dislike to me, and I soon experienced the disciplinary ways first of him and then the other prefects. I think that he had an aversion to my sense of humour and didn't find it funny at all. He chased me all around the school.

The prefects dished out various punishments which may have been detention, or Shakespeare's Hamlet. They carried cards with quotes from Hamlet on them which had to be written out two hundred times at home. Sometimes, a whole group of us would receive the same punishment at the same time. We all lived close to each other so we used to meet up and do it together. Richard often escorted me to Mr JJ O'Brian's headmaster's room to receive the cane. JJ O'Brian was sat at his desk directly opposite the door and he was the first thing to meet my eyes as I entered. It was a foreboding sight. Behind Mr JJ O'Brian's desk, there was a big sash window that let the sunlight in and blinded me, so much sometimes that I was unable to open my eyes and could only hear him speaking. I also visited Mr Taylor's room often. His nickname was Fritz because one of the subjects that he taught was German.

I thought that the education that I received from my new teachers was top quality compared to some of the education from the teachers at William Blake.

I felt that I was being taught at grammar school level because all of the teachers at Sinjun's were of a grammar school standard. The boys that started at Sinjun's before the merge started off as grammar pupils and they were going to finish grammar pupils. Therefore, it was still classed as a grammar school by a lot of people. We were taught to pronounce our words properly. I used to swear when I started the new school, but by the time I left, I had stopped. Nobody really knew how the two merged schools would get on. But everyone in the upper school got on quite well from the off. Maybe it was down to the fact that most of the boys lived in Battersea and knew each other somehow. If anyone wanted to get on that was the perfect opportunity to do so.

There were some things during my school days that I didn't like or agree with. The senior boys liked to round up some of the new boys, take them around to the squash court and throw them in. The seniors piled in after them and shut the door, making it impossible to get out again. They spat upwards at the new boys who were all squashed together like sardines in a tin. Because of this, the caretaker was ordered to use the court as a storage room and fill it with old desks and chairs. In all the time, I was at school I never saw it being used for its intended purpose. Another thing that sticks in my head is when a Sinjun's friend from the estate opposite mine went on a school camping trip. When he came back, some of the other boys from school were teasing him quite badly about it. At the time, we were very good friends in and out of school. I asked him what had happened. I had a shock coming to me as it wasn't anything like the kind of answer that I expected, and it made me feel very sad. The science teacher who taught at Sinjun's had arranged the camping trips had been caught sleeping with a boy. According to some other boys who attended the school, it wasn't the first time that he had engaged in sexual activity with the boy either. The teacher was no longer teaching at the school by the time I attended there because he got suspended.

Both William Blake and Sinjun's had quite strong and successful football teams, and when they merged, there were plenty of talented players. The cream of the crop was picked to make one great team. I believe that the team went on to win a few trophies. Pupils at Sinjun's used the playing fields at Trinity Road for sports activities. It was right next to Wandsworth Common, where we had the opportunity to play cricket in the summer. We stopped using Battersea Park for those events. The school used the football pitches at the playing fields during the winter. In the summer months, we played rounders.

I had quite a lot of stamina and enjoyed cross-country running. I was allowed to meet up with some of the senior boys, and there were about five of us who were all very strong runners. We got changed at the school grounds, which had a wooden hut with changing rooms, before running. We ran at a steady pace down Trinity Road towards Tooting Bec Station and then on towards Streatham Common. The side of the common was steep and it required a bit of effort to push ourselves up the steep hill to the top before running back down again to make the return journey to the playing fields.

We were hot! The changing room would fill with steam that billowed out when we took off our tracksuit bottoms. I had a bit of trouble pacing myself, and sometimes, I felt quite exhausted by the end of the run. The school held a cross-country run for all year groups in the upper school around part of Wandsworth Common. I was now becoming a very strong runner and lapped the teacher who was running with us. I came first in my year and the year above. The only ones that I couldn't beat were the boys that I trained with, but it was a great achievement nevertheless as they had been running for a longer time than me.

Weekends with Steven

During the weekends, I still stayed at Steven's. One of his new hobbies was keeping finches, which he had in his front room in a cage. The cage was five feet high by four feet wide. There were quite a few birds in there. Every night, he covered the cages, otherwise they would twitter and keep everyone awake. Steven also liked to play board games and frequently purchased new ones. One of my favourites was Monopoly, but we also enjoyed playing lots of other popular games together such as Cluedo, chess and draughts. There was another one that I liked. I can't remember for sure what it was called, but I think it was called Auctioneers. The object of the game was to work out how much a painting was worth and then bid on it. One of my most disliked games was called Castle Colditz. None of us really knew how to play it. We tried a few times, but it ended up at the bottom of the pile in the cupboard.

Steven's family originated from Woking. We went there sometimes in the summer for days out. There was a place where we hired rowing boats for the day and row them up and down the river. The river was very narrow with steep banks and there were fields on each side. In one field, there was the ruins of an old castle. As we went down the river, Steven would say 'Look at that!', and before I knew it, I was in the water. He would say to me, "You like to swim." Then he would tell me to swim behind the boat. It was good fun, and I must admit that I did enjoy swimming and Steven's sense of humour. I wonder how many people can say that they swam in a river? I have always enjoyed wild swimming and the outside life. We liked to catch fish by floating empty milk bottles. We tied string around the neck of the bottle and pushed bread inside them before throwing them into the river. I remember there was one time where I threw mine in, but I forgot to hold onto the string. That was me finished early! We caught small fish in the bottles, and it was a fun activity that didn't cost anything. It's true that the most simplest things in life can be so much fun and give the greatest pleasure.

Steven had a small room in his home that he didn't really use because it was too small, so it was only used for storage. One weekend when I went to visit, Steven told me to go and look in the room. I opened the door to find a gleaming orange racing bike! It was called 'Tour de France', and I must say that it was a very good make of bike at the time. It had ten gears and was very smooth to ride. Steven told me that he had bought it for himself but then decided that he didn't want it, after all. He thought that I would like to have it instead. I said yes straightaway. He then told me that I would have to take over the repayments, which weren't actually very much. He acquired it from the Freeman's catalogue, and he handed me the repayment card, which I accepted gracefully. Steven no longer needed to come and collect me from home, and I had the most freedom that I had ever had. I could go wherever I pleased.

Reunion

I had not seen my Aunt Ciss for a couple of years for a couple of reasons. One of the reasons was she couldn't stand to be around David. The other reason that Aunt Ciss had stopped seeing me was because she had been told by Grandad Charlie to stay away from me! I had missed my aunt dearly, and it was about to become apparent that she had missed me too. I took it upon myself to ride my bike to see her and give her a very nice surprise. It was a Saturday morning, and I rode my bike from Battersea to her address in Chancellor Grove, west Dulwich. Aunt Ciss had absolutely no idea that I had decided to visit her, and I was hoping so much that she would be at home.

She lived in a ground floor flat of a house that was owned by Dulwich Council. I remember seeing two bells on the left-hand side of the main door entrance. Aunt Ciss' was the oldest bell, and it was made of Bakelite. The other one was plastic. I pressed the bell and heard it ringing inside the flat. After a short wait, the door opened, and I saw Aunt Ciss standing there, mouth open with a look of surprise on her face. She said to me, "Is that you, Mark?"

I replied with excitement, "It's me, Aunty!" Without any hesitation, she held her arms straight out to me, and I came to her for a hug. I could feel the love coming from her as I lingered in that embrace. It felt so warm and welcoming.

We both had a little cry; the experience was very emotional for both of us and we didn't want to let go. It was as if we hadn't been together for many years. I loved my aunt and she loved me. The love between us was unconditional. She looked unchanged to me, but I must have changed and grown quite a lot during the time that we had been away from each other. I was eagerly invited in, and once I walked through the main front door, I was standing in a small lobby area. There was a door to a first floor flat directly in front of the entrance, but Aunt Ciss' ground floor flat was at the end of the hall on the right side. I parked my bike up against the wall, and we went into her flat. Aunt Ciss had a comfortable home. There was a coat stand to the left of the front door. I noticed that Uncle Ernie's overcoats and hats were proudly on display, and at the bottom of the stand, there was a place for his walking sticks and umbrella. We walked together down the narrow hallway and past the bedroom and front room. Aunt Ciss kept a large photograph of Uncle Ernie on the wall in her bedroom. When she woke, she said good morning to him, and then at bedtime, she said 'Good night, my love' and blew him a kiss. We walked on down the hall and straight into the kitchen where she sat me down next to the gas cooker. She put some milk on the boiler to make me a milky coffee. I didn't like hot milk due to having been given milk in primary school that had been left in the hot sun. It tasted disgusting, and I could not drink hot milk, full stop. But I could tolerate it as a coffee.

We began to catch up on all of the lost time. Aunt Ciss started by asking me what had been happening in my life. I only told her about the good things and never the bad. Even though I was a young boy, I felt that I should protect her from the hurtful and upsetting aspects of my life. The last thing that I wanted to do was make her feel sad. We talked about school, and I informed her about how much better I was getting along. I had really settled down and actually liked school. It was much better than being at home, even if I did get the cane. It didn't really hurt me compared to the beatings that David gave me from time to time.

Aunt Ciss asked me about Mum and how she was doing at that time. Mum was her favourite niece at the time, despite everything that had gone on in the family. They fell out when I was in my twenties and never spoke to one another again. Aunt Ciss was not a silly person, and she was able to figure out most happenings without having all of the facts and details. I asked her about the family members that I was unable to see, such as the Martin family and my Aunt Dolly. I had missed them all, and it was good to hear about them. We ended up having a lengthy conversation. It had been a couple of years since the last time that we spoke, after all. After that, we went into the garden together.

When I had visited as a younger child, we often went outside and into the garden. Aunt Ciss was a very keen gardener. She had 'green fingers' and was able to make everything grow in abundance. When Uncle Ernie was alive, he enjoyed the gardening too, bless him. The garden was only about twelve metres long by six metres wide. But the size of the garden didn't mean that it was dull. There were plants and colourful flowers in neatly dug borders on each side.

93

Uncle Ernie had grown vegetables at the far end of the garden. I noticed that there were still strings of runner beans as well as potatoes in the ground, along with some other veg, which Aunt Ciss continued to look after and use for Sunday lunches. She kept her garden very well, and the grass was mown short and tidy.

When we came back inside the flat, Aunt Ciss and I went to the front room. I noticed that she still had a traditional coal fire. I helped her to prepare it by putting several sheets of screwed up newspaper between the coals before lighting every one of them to make the coals catch fire. Aunt Ciss then opened up one of the newspaper sheets and covered the entire opening of the fireplace. The flue pulled the air through the bottom of the grill where the coals were situated and created a draught. This made the coals catch fire very quickly, and I remember it to be a bit scary sometimes when the newspaper that was being held caught alight! Once the coals were burning sufficiently, we stoked the fire. Aunt Ciss had two armchairs in the room, which she moved until they were facing the fireplace. I was allowed to sit in the armchair that was closest to the fire. We had afternoon tea and a sandwich each, which had been neatly cut into four squares. I stayed there for most of the afternoon and time seemed to have flown by. I left to go home before it became dark outside and harder to ride the bike. We hugged one more time at the door and said our goodbyes. That was hard for both of us. I told Aunt Ciss that I would come again and she replied, "See you soon, then."

After that initial encounter, I visited Aunt Ciss most weeks. If I went to see her on a Sunday, she always cooked me a delicious roast, and I liked to help out by picking the veg for her at the bottom of the garden. Sometimes, she asked me to cut the grass for her. The lawnmower was stored in a small brick shed at the end of the building. I always happily obliged. It felt nice to be able to do something for her. It must have been about three weeks after my first visit when I decided to go and see Aunt Ciss again. I rang the front doorbell and waited for her to answer. She came to the door and stood there looking me up and down whilst shaking her head slowly side to side. She told me to put my bike in the lobby and leave my coat on. Aunt Ciss then put on her own coat and silk scarf and beckoned me to go with her.

Her flat wasn't too far from Norwood High Street. It was like any other high street with food shops, newsagents, hardware shops, a couple of men's boutique shops and a very good shoe shop that was situated close to the train station on the opposite side of the road. We walked along the street almost in silence. Aunt Ciss hardly said a word to me the whole time that we were walking, and neither I to her. We got to the shops, and she ushered me straight into one of the men's boutique shops. I pushed the door open, and we went inside. Aunt Ciss looked around in quiet contemplation before pointing at a shirt that was on display. She asked me if I liked it. I replied, "Yes, I do." She then told me to go to the small changing room at the back of the shop and remove all of my clothes. I did as I was told. No sooner had I done so, Aunt Ciss proceeded to pass me clothing items through the side of the curtain. An entire outfit; pants, socks, shirt, tie and trousers. She simply told me, "Put these on." I have to admit, I looked far more smarter than I had done when we entered the shop. The clothes that I had just removed looked like rags in comparison. I didn't have a smile on my face, like people usually do when they get new things. I should have been like a kid when they get a new toy. Instead, my expression was one of sadness because my aunt must have felt as if she had to do that for me. I felt as if she had clothed me in herkindness.

After the purchase was completed, we walked out of the shop and she took my hand. I was directed up towards the station. We crossed to the other side of the road and into the shoe shop. Aunt Ciss told me to choose a pair of shoes. I pointed at the black classic Kempton shoes with tassels. She didn't hesitate to tell the shop assistant that she wanted to buy them. The hand-me-down shoes that I was already wearing were too big for me. I had shoved cotton wool down the toes to make them smaller. They were good leather shoes despite being too big. Mum provided me with shoes, but they were often cheap and made with synthetic uppers that cracked and peeled off. I appreciated the decent shoes. After that, we went back to the flat to have dinner.

I never asked Aunt Ciss what had motivated her to buy me an entire new outfit, but I was very grateful that she did. The new clothes and shoes didn't only make me look better, they made me feel better inside. It had been a long time since I had looked so smart and tidy. Mum would always buy me long school trousers and take them up with wonder web. Then when I grew taller, she undid the wonder web, lowered the length and hemmed them again with the wonder web. By the time my trousers actually fitted me properly, they looked tired and worn out. Aunt Ciss was not happy that Grandad Charlie never thought to buy me new clothes every now and again. Instead, he moaned at my mother about it. He knew that Mum didn't have the money to buy them for me herself, and it didn't make sense that he left her to struggle like that. Aunt Ciss thought that if Grandad really cared about my appearance like he made out, that he should have taken me to buy some new clothes every now and then. Things like that were always left to Hilda. Hilda was the one who wrote out all of the Christmas and birthday cards too. She always put a five pound note in mine. By now, Christmas and birthdays was the only time that I saw Grandad and Hilda. Mum and I hardly ever went to visit them.

Discovering My Sports Interests

Steve started football training in a local school on Wednesday nights, playing five-a-side football in the school gym. Steve asked me if I wanted to do it and I said yes. Because I would be playing against men who were twice my age. I needed to get a letter from the school to do so. I only sat and watched the first time that I went, but I liked the look of it very much and couldn't wait to start. I went to the headmaster, Mr JJ O'Brian, to get permission to take part, and he wrote me out a consent letter. I played very well, and during the games, I won a lot of ball. I felt as if I was just as good a player as the men I was playing alongside and against. For that brief time in my life, I could have taken up football and played more seriously in team games. I even played two games for the school, but I couldn't get on with the boys in the school team. They always made me feel as if I wasn't as good as them, like the underdog. So I stopped.

In the same year, I began to play rugby at school. The teachers that coached rugby were all rugby players themselves and played for clubs. We trained at rugby fields next to Richmond Park, just off of the A3 road. Another place that we trained at was Raynes Park rugby pitch. One of the rugby teachers was a man called TI Jones and the other teacher was Mr Harris. TI Jones also taught at the P.E. lessons. We played a lot of basketball in P.E. I learned how to throw the basketball into the basket from a distance and became very good at scoring. TI Jones showed me how to use weights properly too. In the gym, we had a wooden climbing frame which was pulled out from the wall. It had ropes attached to it which we could climbup.

The gym was also used as the school dining area. Lots of tables and chairs were brought in and set out with four chairs to each table. The school used dinner tokens which could be purchased from two machines outside the school office. The boys who received free school meals obtained their dinner tokens from the office. When David was not in work, I got free school meals, but when he was working, I had to take sandwiches. I preferred the dinners to sandwiches. A lot of the boys went out of school at lunchtime because they didn't like the food at school. They often went to the chippy on the high street so they didn't want their tokens. But they did want to swap their tokens for my sandwiches so that they could eat the sandwiches at breaktime. That suited me fine. At the drive-in entrance to the school, the boys played Penny Up or Pitching Pennies. Players took turns to throw a coin at a wall from a distance. The coin that landed closest to the wall was the winner. This area was out of bounds to the boys, as well as the courtyard that it led onto. This was another way that I obtained tokens for school dinners. I absolutely loathed having sandwiches. They played with two penny coins, which got scratched up by the floor. If any of the boys got caught with a pocketful of coins like that, the teacher would know for sure that they had been gambling.

Rugby was going well and us boys had now played a few games against each other by splitting up into two teams. None of us had ever played rugby before so we had a lot to learn. The rules were very different to how they are now, and many injuries occurred. I remember that TI Jones was the teacher on this day when there was a bit of a bundle, and the boy who was at the bottom of the bundle was holding his hand in his other hand when TI Jones got to him. The boy raised his arm and his bone was poking through his skin. It was an open fracture, which is quite a serious injury. TI Jones looked at him and said 'you'll be all right' when he knew full well that he wouldn't and needed to go to hospital. I remember another occasion where I was standing quite close to the touchline when a boy from the opposing team came running at me with the ball. As he came closer to me, I put my arm straight out horizontally and it came into contact with the boy's neck. He came to an immediate halt. His feet lifted up in front of him and the back of his head hit the ground very hard.

The boy was out cold and unresponsive for quite some time. TI Jones was not very happy with my conduct, but he let me off without a reprimand because we had only just started to learn the game. He told me never to do that again. We used to be a mixed lot of boys from both William Blake and Sinjun's, but as one united school, we got on well together. All Sinjun's alike and on the same side when we started to play against other schools. I have to admit that our side didn't always play by the rules as the other side found out. We learned as we went along and I put that down to TI Jones and Mr Harris, who did a lot of coaching. Sometimes, we would train up at our school fields in Trinity Road. I had gotten right into rugby and knew that it was the game for me. I stopped playing football and even stopped watching matches on telly. I watched more rugby games and wanted to learn everything about the game, which I did.

Retribution

Back at school, there was a rumour going around amongst the boys about the science teacher that had taken some of the boys camping in the summer. Word was he had been allowed back into the school to teach. None of the boys were pleased about his return, and I think that a lot of the teachers felt the same way too. By today's rules and standards, he would have been struck off for good, but things were not so strict back then. I took a personal offence to his presence because my friend had attended that camping trip, and he had put up with kids taking the mick out of him ever since. It had only been a few weeks since the teacher's return back to school. I was in the science lab alone with him whilst he was putting some books away. I couldn't stand the sight of him and could feel my rage building up inside, like a kettle about to go onto full boil.

As the teacher was walking into the cupboard, I swiftly kicked him in the back. He was a man of short stature so it had been easy to do. The teacher tumbled forwards and hit his head on the wall in front of him. I briefly looked at him as he stood shocked and disorientated, then I locked him inside the cupboard. I should have just walked away but didn't finish there. I opened up some of the drawers on the science lab tables that contained the Bunsen burners. Next, I screwed up sheets of paper and filled the drawers, then I lit the Bunsen burners whilst making them face the drawers. Lastly, I exited the science lab and locked the door behind me. With my heart thumping hard in my chest, I ran down the stairs from the science labs. Mr Taylor's office was right next to the stairs and, as I got to the bottom of them, he hurried out. We could both hear the teacher shouting from the locked cupboard. Mr Taylor told me to wait in his office and ran swiftly up the stairs towards the teacher's shouts for help.

When Mr Taylor returned to his office, he was more than displeased with me. He didn't even ask me what I had done wrong, but I knew what to expect next as I had been disciplined by him on several occasions before. He picked up his cane, then ordered me to bend over his desk and lift the back of my blazer up. He took the first strike, and then another, but the second strike missed my backside and the cane came right up my back. I said, "Sir, do you want to take it again?" Which he did. He was absolutely fuming. I took my punishment honourably, and it was worth it. That was the end of the situation.

Kids never seemed to get sent home or expelled in those days. It must have had to be extremely bad for that to happen. On another occasion, one of the boys was sitting at his desk in his class in the science building when another boy hit him around the back of the head with a book. The boy who had been hit spun around very quickly to retaliate, but he didn't realise that the science teacher was then standing directly behind him. His clenched fist caught the teacher in the jaw. The unfortunate boy was then taken down by the school reverend to his cubbyhole, which was situated under the stairs that led to the library. The teacher gave him six of the best, but on the last one, the boy laughed out loud, so he took it upon himself to give him another six. These were done with much harder strokes, which was illegal. They were only allowed to give a maximum of six. The boy took the situation up with Mr Taylor who asked him if he thought that the teacher should be expelled for his actions. The boy replied no because he thought that the rest of the teachers would give him a hard time from thereon in. He asked Mr Taylor to let it go; however, I know that the incident has had a profound and lasting effect, even into his adult life.

None of the students were happy that the science teacher was still allowed to teach at the school. One afternoon, a revenge attack took place. As soon as the bell went to signal the end of the school day, all of us boys from William Blake and Sinjun's formed two lines. The lines started on each side of the footpath from the science building main doors, continued through the courtyard and then carried on throughout the main building. They continued further through the big main entrance doors and on to the science teacher's car which was parked about a hundred yards away. We were ready and waiting for the teacher to leave the science building.

The teacher came through the doors and walked along the path that was flanked by boys on both sides. We all took turns to spit on him. He didn't try to run but continued to walk very gingerly through the middle of us all. By the time the teacher got to his car, it had also been spat upon. It was vandalised as well for good measure. The window wipers were broken off, the tyres had been let down and the boys had made sure that it had a really good covering of phlegm. There weren't any other school staff members in sight. Sadly, our attempts to intimidate the teacher were not enough to make him leave the school permanently. He had a couple of days off and then returned. What a nightmare!

Playground Shooting

One sunny school day, the P.E. teacher decided that we should play football in the playground. We prepared for the lesson by putting on our white shorts and plimsolls in the changing rooms before going into the playground, then we were split into two equal teams. We spread out all over the playground, and the game started. It was going really well, and I even managed to get the ball. I was quite close to the squash court building when I heard a loud sound like a shot coming out of an air rifle. We all began to run in sheer panic in every direction. As I looked behind me towards the place where the noise came from, I heard another loud bang echoing across the playground.

There was a block of old council flats with very big sash windows in the general direction of where the bangs were coming from. I noticed that the window right in the middle of the block was wide open. A man was standing there reloading his air rifle in preparation to fire it again! In a shock moment, I realised that he was aiming his gun at us boys in the playground. The gunman managed to shoot a boy standing at the top end of the playground in his thigh. Everyone ran away from the playground for cover very quickly. Some of us managed to hide behind the squash court until it was safe to come out again.

Someone from the school telephoned the police about the incident, and they responded quickly. The police went straight to the man's flat to apprehend him. They were unable to find the air rifle at first, but one of the officers had the notion to take a look up into the old fireplace chimney. He put his hand up it to feel around inside and discovered the air rifle tucked up in the corner. The gunman was escorted away to the police station and charged. The flats were being used by squatters and most of them were empty. I believe that they were boarded up for some time and then sold to a private developer before being sold again as individual flats.

Lab Incident

I started to learn chemistry in the lab on the top floor of the science building, and the teacher's name was Mr Beanland. He liked to carry out experiments, some of which seemed as if they were really dangerous. There was one particular experiment that he liked to show the boys. He filled balloons with helium and then attached a long string to the knot end. The string was soaked in petroleum. More balloons meant a bigger bang. On one occasion, Mr Beanland used a lot more balloons than he normally did. He put the bunch of balloons outside of the window of the lab that faced the playground and used a wooden stick to push them away from it. When he let them go, the balloons floated up to the height of the top of the window. Finally, he lit the string and the flames began to travel hastily up the string towards the balloons.

All of a sudden, an unexpected gust of wind wafted the balloons close to the window again! We knew what was coming next so we all turned away and crouched down in anticipation of the inevitable. There was an almighty gas explosion that shattered the top window. The force of the explosion could be felt and it was so loud! Small pieces of glass showered the vicinity. Fortunately, nobody was hurt. I imagine that the bang could have been heard from quite a distance away. At the time, I'm not sure that all of the boys realised the severity of this incident. I'm not aware of what the consequence was for Mr Beanland, but I think that the school disallowed him from carrying out that experiment ever again.

Apart from that, Mr Beanland was a very good teacher; in fact, I found all of my teachers to be very good at educating. A lot of the boys in my year had passed their 11+ exam. When the schools merged together, we became a mixed ability year, but the school was still teaching to a grammar school standard. Because of this, I had homework every night, and there was stricter discipline with more punishment. My maths teacher was particularly stern. If a boy was not paying attention in class, they got the chalk in their head. He always managed to hit his target. We all knew that as soon as the chalk hit our head, we would have a lot of homework to do, and believe me when I say that it was a lot! Despite his draconian ways, he was a good maths teacher, better than the maths teacher at William Blake. Due to his teaching, my maths skills became very good.

Running

It was 1979 and a year had passed since I left what is now known as the lower school. We didn't do cycling at Crystal Palace any more. But I was playing rugby, sailing, canoeing, taking part in cross-country running and playing cricket. During the summer months, schools met up at Hurlingham Stadium in Fulham. It had a running track and schools met there to compete against each other. I took part in some of the races, for instance, the 1500-metre race. It was a hard race to compete in because runners had to know the right pace. If they peaked too early, they would lose. Some of the very good runners had proper track running shoes with spikes. I was never afforded the luxury of a pair of those shoes. I only had the running shoes that I used for street running. This put me at a disadvantage straightaway.

I started running on a regular basis, either before or after school. If I went for a run in the morning, I got up early at six o'clock. I started by running up to Lavender Hill from my flat and then on towards Queenstown Road. The right turn into Queenstown Road was quite long and steep. At the top, there was a set of traffic lights that went into a T junction to Clapham Common, which was directly ahead. I then proceeded to run left towards Old Town and stay on the outside of the common, all the way around and back to Queenstown Road, back down to Lavender Hill then back to where I started at Shirley Grove. This was the longest run that I had done so far, and I ran it three times a week.

I was still having trouble with pacing myself in a run. I had competed in a few runs up at the common whilst running at Queenstown Road during the same time period. There was another male runner who wore a light blue tracksuit and ran in the opposite direction to me. He stood out because he was taller than me with blonde hair, and we passed each other on several occasions. It was in the summertime and very early in the morning. There was nobody else around. On the third occasion that I noticed the runner in the blue tracksuit, he was running in the same direction as me, up Queenstown Road towards

Clapham Common. As I turned the corner from Queenstown Road, he came from the opposite corner, and we started to run together.

We struck up a conversation, and I ran alongside the man all the way around the common. I told the man that I had a problem with pacing myself so he explained to me how I could get over it and make my running a lot better. He also told me that he wore two black bin bags underneath his tracksuit whilst running to get a good sweat up. He told me that it was to aid weight loss and build muscle mass. I started to wear the black bags, too. We ran a few more times together, but after that, he never seemed to be around, and I didn't see him again. I enjoyed running because it gave me time to gather my thoughts about the things that were going on in my life at the time and helped me to feel at peace with myself. I continued to run solo three times a week for many years.

Clapham Common

I went out with my friends on our bikes to Clapham Common in the summertime. The whole of the common had a load of pitches on it. Some were used for playing a game called rugby netball and others were for rugby league and Gaelic football. I was interested in all of them, but it was the rugby netball that intrigued me the most. I loved to go to the common at about seven o'clock in the evening and watch the games. As I watched, I learned how to play too. I stood and watched the entire game. Rugby netball was very different from rugby union, which I had really gotten into on a school level. I was always playing competitively for the school. I knew for sure that rugby netball was the game for me and couldn't wait until I was old enough to take part myself. I was glad that it wouldn't be long.

The game was played on a full-sized football pitch. It had the same layout as a football pitch, but the goal was a post just over three metres high with a huge hoop and net on the top of it for players to score a basket. A rugby ball was used and players could throw the ball forwards or behind them. Kicking the ball was not permitted. A penalty was awarded to the opposite side if that ever happened. It was a very fast game as the ball was passed around the pitch, pretty much like a football is passed around with feet. It was one-to-one tackling where players could try to get the ball from their opponents, even if they were both on the ground. Instead of taking penalty a goal, the player stood on a spot inside the penalty area and took a shot at the net. There wasn't a scrum down to restart a game. Instead, the referee put the ball down between a player from each side, whilst the other players stood a little further back from them. It was down to the two players either side of the ball to try to capture it first. After watching a game, I would make my way home, but I didn't go straight home. I liked to stay out and play with the other kids in my area until it was time to go in.

David's Anger

One Saturday afternoon, I was coming down the communal staircase in my flat block to go outside. Just before I reached the bottom, David started to come up the stairs towards me. He was wearing a three-piece suit and looking in a rough state. The suit jacket was quite badly ripped from the collar to the arm and his hair was a scruffy mess. I noticed that he had bruising on his face too. David had been drinking in the local pub in Lavender Hill. I found it quite amusing to see David looking so dishevelled. It made me feel happy inside to see that someone had given him a taste of his own medicine. He looked at me and caught me grinning at him. From the look on his face, I could tell that he was not happy about this, not one bit!

David had got himself into a fight with the boyfriend of the girl who lived on the ground floor. He was a fireman and much fitter than David was. David had stupidly made an advance towards the man's girlfriend. As a consequence, he endured the full force of the man's rage. He had really hurt David. The girlfriend was the one that had previously helped me with my artwork. I thought that David had been dealt everything that he deserved.

More fool him for trying to take advantage of her! Catching me sniggering about it was an added insult to David's injury, and he didn't hesitate for very long before he got his own back on me for it with nothing but pure spite.

I returned home from school another afternoon in the following week, and as I came in through the front door, I saw that David was waiting there for me. I could tell by the expression on his face that it wasn't to be a friendly encounter by any means. As soon as I was inside and the front door was closed, he marched me to my bedroom. He then pointed to the built-in wardrobe and a small speck of paint that I had accidentally smeared onto it whilst doing my oil painting. Then he urgently pointed out two more places in the room where I had managed to spill a little paint. I had gotten used to David's irrational behaviour, but I never could have guessed what was coming next. He gleefully opened the top door of the cupboard where I kept all of my art things and said in a sarcastic tone, "You won't be doing any more painting in this house!" It was completely empty! To my dismay, David had removed all of my brushes, oil paints and paper that I did my paintings on. He had thrown them all away.

Well, I wasn't grinning anymore, and I must have had a face like thunder. This appeared to please David immensely. He had not only got back at me in one of the most callous ways imaginable but also the girl downstairs who had helped me to do the paintings. He knew that by hurting me like that he would hurt her too, as we were very good friends. The girl and I had very good chit-chat between ourselves when we were together, and we remained very good friends for the whole time that I lived in Shirley Grove. But David must have still been pissed off because, shortly after throwing away all of my art materials, he started picking on me again.

David knew how much I loved building and taking pride in my Airfix models. I had amassed quite a lot of them and proudly displayed them all around my bedroom. It was a nice summer's day when I walked cheerfully to my bedroom and saw David in there, with the window wide open. It took me by surprise as I had not expected him in there at all. I noticed that half of my planes were no longer on display and that David had stacked them up on the window ledge. He looked towards me with a spiteful grin and said, "Shall we see if these can fly?" He started to throw them out of the window, one by one. We lived on the second floor and, even though there was a grass verge at the bottom, all of the planes broke in one way or another.

David's actions really pissed me off, and I was at the end of my tether with his wicked, bullying ways. I got two of Mum's black bags from the kitchen and went downstairs to pick the broken pieces up. I filled both of the bags right up and took them to the rubbish bins in the block. It had taken me years to build the planes, tanks and one or two ships. I thought about all of the patience that I had given them whilst I was alone in my own space and time. David sure did get his own back on me for my smugness on the day that he got beaten up. I imagine that he thought that he could just carry on beating and mentally abusing me. But I could feel then that the day where I would make him stop was coming very soon.

Bordering Maturity

My first concert experience was at the Rainbow Theatre in Findsbury Park. It was May 1979, and my friend Wendy invited me to go with her to see the Jamaican Reggae artist, Dennis Brown. At the time, Dennis owned a small record shop in Clapham Junction. We had such a fun time. The experience overwhelmed me with joy! When the concert finished, we made our way to the West End to meet with Wendy's mother. I can't remember the reason why, but they weren't going back to Battersea. I walked all the way home, alone. It was early hours of the morning when a policeman encountered me on Lavender Hill and crossed the road towards me. He asked me why I was out so late alone and where I was going. He seemed satisfied with my answer and offered to walk me home to the top of my road. It was around 2:30 AM when I got back to Shirley Grove, but I didn't mind. I had had a great night. Wendy and I didn't see much of each other as we grew older. She met other boys, I met other girls and we naturally went our separate ways.

Around this time, our home life changed quite a lot. Mum and David had another baby that year. She was born on 9 July 1979, and they called her Clair. She had blonde hair and blue eyes and slept in a cot with Mum and David in their bedroom. A new baby in the home didn't really change very much. David still drank to excess and spent a lot of time in the pub.

David had an uncle called Fred. Fred was in the pub every night and was a true alcoholic. I can't remember why, but Fred had nowhere to live and David invited him to stay with us. Despite his love for drink, Fred was a pleasant man who never had much conversation in him. There were two single beds in my room so David offered Fred the other one to sleep in. Fred drank so much I could smell the stale beer leeching out of his skin. It made his clothes stink too. As a consequence, my room smelled really badly all of the time. I was always in bed asleep when Fred came home from the pub. But when he came in, he woke me up with his presence. I pulled my bedcovers over my head, not only because of the smell but also because of his snoring. It was loud and kept me awake for half of the night. It wasn't long before the smell of alcohol went right through the flat. During the daytime, Mum opened my bedroom windows in an attempt to get rid of the horrible stench. But it just stayed there as it seemed to have soaked into the walls and furniture. Fred stayed with us for a few months before he managed to find a new place and move out. Trust me when I say that I didn't miss him one bit.

At school, we had a big game coming up against Emmanuel School. This school was well established for its teaching and very well known for rugby. They won the majority of their games against rival schools. The time had come for our chance to compete against them. Everybody had a position and mine was almost always on the wing, though sometimes I played in the pack as hooker due to my size and my ability of hooking a ball back in a scrum. A month before we were due to play this game, I had gone to school with flu-like symptoms, and I felt rough all day.

I had a close friend at school called Lewis. We had quite a long friendship because we had both started school at William Blake at the same time. We were also in the same class and, in later years at Sinjun's, we took a majority of the same subjects. We spent a great deal of time together out of school, during the week and at weekends. One day, I was walking with a couple of other boys through the courtyard at school from one building to another. Lewis came flying out of the main school door and straight into me, knocking my books out of my hands. The other boys around me said that I ought to have a fight with Lewis. All fights were strictly kept away from school grounds, otherwise the consequence was the cane. So after school, we went to a small playground that was not far from our school. It had started to rain, but there were still a lot of boys hanging about to watch as the word had gotten out. They started chanting and edging Lewis and I on to fight. We started by throwing punches at each other, which were very soft and didn't really hurt. Neither of us threw a punch above the shoulders, and it was over very quickly. We stopped and went our separate ways.

A couple of the Sinjun boys thought that I was a wuss and that I couldn't fight. How wrong they were! Lewis was one of my best friends and there was no way that I was going to hurt him for their entertainment and amusement. I had never had a fight during my time at Sinjun's so they never got to find out my abilities. The next day, Lewis and I had put the fight behind us and were talking again. In the running up to the game with Emmanuel School, there were certain boys who would not pick me for their side or play on my side, even in badminton. I was not very bothered about it because I knew when to have a fight and when to back off. In my opinion, this made me the better person.

Picking Subjects

I had reached the stage in my schooling where I had to pick subjects. The compulsory ones were English and maths. The additional ones that I chose were physics, electronics, woodwork, metalwork, technical drawing and motor mechanics. To keep track of school period and where we had to be, we made a timetable on a card. These periods varied in time with most being for one hour, however, some were for two hours or even a whole afternoon. This meant that I hardly ever spent the full day with the same boys as we all had our own set of subjects and timetables. It took me some time to get used to the changes, and at first, I was late for the odd class. But over time, I became used to the new routine. I liked learning all of the subjects that I had chosen, but technical drawing was the subject that I enjoyed the most.

Our teacher was a well-spoken man with the attire to match. He wore a double-breasted blazer which was grey in colour and highly polished shoes. He was a likeable teacher who communicated with us really well and had a good way of making us understand the subject. I was expected to have my own clutch pencils, compasses in various sizes, a scale rule, drafting triangles, French Ship Flexible drafting curve tools as well as a drawing board which I did my homework on. Everyone in the class helped each other out and got along well. It didn't matter which of the two merged schools we came from. This lesson was held on the first floor. On the stairwell, there were old, cast iron radiators and one happened to be right outside the classroom. One of the boy's favourite pranks was to find big fat crayons and place them on top of the radiator. They melted slowly and the sticky, colourful mess ran down the back of the radiator. Everyone knew when someone had done this because of the distinct smell. It drove the teachers mad because they could never catch the culprits no matter how hard they tried!

In the motor mechanics workshop, there was an old Morris Minor motorcar that we worked on. We also travelled to Wandsworth College, which was situated on the one-way system near the Town Hall, to learn in the workshop there. Electronics was taught in the science building. We learned how to make circuit boards and how to solder resistors and other components onto them. We got the opportunity to make our own radios, which I did and was allowed to take home once completed. It was great fun to make something like that and then see it fully working. Woodwork and metalwork were taught in two old, wooden cabins that sat back-to-back. They had been there for years. The metalwork shop area was a fair size. Inside there was a metalwork lathe, a fox drill that was on a stand for drilling metal plates, benches and a fire area for warming metal.

There were also hand tools such as hammers, an anvil and a chisel. It is fair to say that it was well equipped. The woodwork shop had the distinct smell of freshly sawn timber. There were several types of timber around the room, which wasn't as big as the metalwork room. However, it was adequate enough to carry out the type of work that we were doing. I liked and got along well with the teacher that taught both of these subjects. He was a good teacher and knew his stuff. He taught with passion and always took the time to listen. He spoke in a manner that required attention, in a good way. He also loved his sports and always used to turn up at Hurlingham when there was running going on against other schools. He would always egg me on to do well in a race on the track.

I was doing very well in all of my subjects. I think that this was down to the fact that I had chosen the subjects that I liked to do and found them all very interesting. I couldn't see the point of wasting brain space on subjects that I didn't like. I did enjoy history but decided not to continue studying it. I would go on to enjoy and learn more about history later on in my life. I still find the subject very interesting to this day. I was a model student and gave full commitment to my studies. I always completed my homework on time.

The Mud Bath

The day had come for the match against Emmanuel School. By now, everyone was playing pretty well. The main thing was that we were playing as a team and watching out for each other on the pitch. We knew our positions and were ready to give it our all! We made our way to Emmanuel School by bus in the afternoon. By the time we got to the school gate, it had started to drizzle with rain. The sky was darkened by thick, grey clouds, but that wasn't enough to dampen our spirits. The entrance with its black iron gates was flanked by brick pillars. The road from the main entrance to the main school building was fairly long and lined with trees. There were fields on the far side, away from the school buildings.

The main building was pretty impressive. The changing rooms were in a building at the end and quite close to the field that we were about to play our match on. Leaves in autumnal hues had fallen from the trees and covered the ground around us. By the time we had got changed into our kit, the sky was much darker and it had started to rain hard. The field that we were about to play on had become very soft and wet with massive puddles forming all over the pitch. We all noticed that the boys on the opposing side were much bigger than we were, but it didn't make us nervous. It made me feel more determined! They had never lost a game so you could say that they were a very drilled side.

The rain was absolutely teeming down when we walked out onto the pitch. So much so that it was difficult for me to see the other players. I played in the back row in this match. We started the game; they won a lot of ball. As it started coming out to their backs, we were waiting for them. We took every one of Emmanuel School's players down with hard tackles. There were only a few punches thrown in a bid to slow them down. It worked. Some of them didn't get up very quickly. The referee could hardly see the tackles or punches going in due to the bad weather conditions. The earth was soddened and the pitch had become extremely muddy. In no time at all, both teams were absolutely

116

covered, and it was difficult to distinguish one person from another. The rain and mud also made the ball very slippery and almost impossible to hold on to. This meant that we couldn't kick the ball very far up the field as it gave the opposition more chance for possession of the ball and the ball wasn't kicked off of the pitch for line outs very often. The ball was kept mainly in one's hands with short passes between team members. No conversions were scored on that tempestuous day as it was almost impossible to control the ball.

That was my first game in which the rain fell constantly throughout. The opposing team scored only a few tries, so by the time the game was over, they didn't win by very much. Emmanuel School had a communal bath which was ready for us when we got back. We all ended up in it with our muddy boots on, and as the mud on those boots dissolved into the water, it produced a thick, earthy soup. It even had lumps of turf floating on the top. But nobody minded about that, and I was grateful that I didn't have to clean my boots before the next match. Every one of us was happy with how the game went and how it would give the other side something to remember us by. The two boys who had called me a wuss when I fought my friend, Lewis, had found a new kind of respect for me. They held their hands out and we shook. They never called me names again.

Enough Is Enough

One afternoon after playing a match, I was at home, sitting on the sofa in the front room. It had been quite a physical game, and I had bruising all down my left side. It was sore, and I was suffering quite a lot of discomfort since the bruising had started to come out. David came home and sat himself on the right side of the sofa next to me. He had been in the pub for all of that afternoon and was a little bit tipsy. He was very close to me, and I could smell the sickly sweet scent of stale alcohol and tobacco. I immediately sensed that David was in one of his bullying moods. He must have been able to see that I was in pain from the expression on my face. With a spiteful grin on his face, David started to prod me forcefully with his fingers, right into my side.

As I instinctively moved away, David got nearer and pushed harder. He was definitely getting something out of inflicting pain on me. I told him to stop touching my side and pushing his fingers into me. Somehow, he was managing to find the tender spots even though he could not see them. David asked me, "Why do you play that silly game?" His breath reeked as he spoke. "It's not for you." He carried on pressing his fingers into my flesh. Something inside of me told me that enough was enough. I was fifteen, also much stronger and built up than I used to be. I got up quickly from the sofa and stood directly in front of David. He must have felt a certain amount of threat as he sat in the sofa beneath me because he went to stand up. But I shook my fist at him, and he stayed seated. Even in his alcoholic state, he must have realised that challenging me was a bad move. I was no longer willing to tolerate David's spiteful taunts. I told him that I had had enough of him bullying me and then I ran out, taking my bike with me.

I rode my bike so fast all the way to David's sister's home in Stockwell. Throughout the journey, I played the event back in my mind over and over. I knew that the day would come, and I didn't have any regrets about my reaction to David's cruel behaviour. I didn't feel the emotions that someone might expect to feel in my situation. I was pretty numb to it, to be honest. I did think that there might be some kind of comeback later on, but I wasn't particularly bothered. The memories of all the things that David had done to me were there, but this was my day of reckoning.

I told David's sister what had happened. She had a phone at home, but we never had the luxury of one at ours. That meant that there was no way for either of us to tell Mum or David where I was. After a few hours, I had calmed down, and David's sister said that it should be all right for me to go home again. I accepted her judgement, and we said our goodbyes. I rode back slowly as I was in no rush to get back. When I got in, Mum was there and so was David. I didn't know what I expect, but it was calm. David didn't say a single word to me about what had happened earlier that day. He knew that I wasn't going to stand for his abusive ways any more. From that day forward, he never laid a finger on me.

Earning for Myself

I started to look for a small job to do, like a paper round. Lots of boys had these jobs, and it was very hard to get one. There was a local chemist store that I knew of where the pharmacist was looking for someone to fill the shelves and serve customers. I was fortunate to get the job and worked for two hours in the evening. I learned how to use the till and worked really hard, but the money wasn't very good. It was better than nothing though. I only stayed there for a short time before they let me go. I had to look for another part time job, but I found one quite quickly and, fortunately for me, it was really close to where I lived. There was a small cafe on Lavender Hill that needed someone to do the washing up so I went to meet the owner for a chat. There weren't any dishwashing machines in those days. Everything had to be washed by hand. It was a family-owned business and the owner seemed like a good person. We got along really well, and he decided to give me the job, after school every evening for two hours.

After school, I went home and changed out of my uniform and into my clothes that I played out in. I made my way to the cafe, which was right next door to the fish and chip shop that my family used. I went straight into the small kitchen that was situated at the back of the shop, behind the counter and up four stairs. The kitchen had a narrow half door so that the food could be passed easily to the waiting staff. It was adequately equipped with a hot service area to the right for cooking eggs, bacon and omelettes, etcetera. There were grills on the same side that heated pots of foods such as beans, peas and greens. Customers could purchase a variety of meals from full English breakfasts in the morning to a roast dinner in the afternoon.

I noticed that there were a lot of single men who came in to eat at the cafe on a regular basis, having worked all day they came in after five o'clock for full dinners. I got to know the regulars well. On the counter, there was a massive tea urn. I couldn't tell you how many cups of tea were poured for the customers over the space of a day. It was a lot though, for almost everyone drank it. Only a few opted for coffee instead. On the left side of the kitchen, there was a worktop and, of course, the sink. This was my area where I washed and dried everything. When there wasn't much to do, I went outside into the backyard and into a small room that was attached to the main building. A couple of dustbins were kept in there, however, they weren't used for storing rubbish; they were for storing potatoes after they had been washed and cut by the machines to make chips. They were done for the shop next door as there were family connections between them.

The man who owned the cafe was called Michael. He and his wife worked very hard at their business. I found him very pleasant to work for. It wasn't very long after I started working in the evenings when he asked me if I wanted to work an eight-hour shift on Saturdays too. I gladly accepted the £1 per hour wage that he offered me, meaning that I was earning £18 per week. The chef and I got along really well. He was a bit of a character and could always make me laugh. He taught me how to cook a wide variety of meals. In the end, I became a bit of an all-rounder; making tea, cooking, washing up, making chips and serving customers. It was hard work, but I didn't mind because they were good people to work for. On Saturdays, after the busy lunch period, the chef always cooked me a very good meal like lamb and rice or steak. Michael allowed me to have dinner as part of my payment and the money that I received helped me immensely.

Time at Sinjun's

Without transportation, it was quite a long walk to school, and if I was late leaving home for any reason, I had to run the whole way there. To save time and energy, many of the boys that I knew rode their bikes and some of the older ones had motorbikes. If we wanted to ride a bike to school, we had to take a cycling proficiency exam. It was held in the school playground during the summer holidays and lasted for a week. I went along with other boys who also wanted to use their bikes. We were taught about road safety and how to keep ourselves safe whilst on the road. The examiners set up courses with orange cones for us to ride between. I found those courses easy, and I was feeling really confident about my ability by the second-to-last day.

The session had just finished, and we were out of the school grounds. I was so pleased with myself that I rode my bike with no hands. In fact, my hands were both above my head, up high, waving from side-to-side. Then, unbeknown to me, the two examiners came out of the school and caught me out! I heard a shout from behind and turned around to the direction of where the examiners were standing. One said to me that I had just failed the exam. This meant that I would not be able to ride my bike to and from school. Not only that, it was the first thing that I had ever failed. I did feel disappointed but didn't dwell on it too much. I knew that it was my own fault and shrugged it off. I continued to walk to school with my friends, just like I always had done.

The weather in the wintertime was sometimes very harsh. The snow fell heavy and settled on the ground, sometimes more than three inches deep. We didn't have the luxury of central heating at home. There was just a fire in the front room and a couple of Calor Gas heaters placed in the hallway to warm the rest of the flat up. On winter mornings, it was so cold indoors that I could see my breath when I exhaled. I leapt out of bed and rushed to get dressed as quickly as I was able to. I always seemed to have a cough and a runny nose in the winter. Maybe this was because I was outside in most weathers. The milkman did his delivery early, way before people were awake in the morning. The air was so cold outside that it made the frozen milk pop out of the top of the bottles before people had the opportunity to bring them inside. The majority of people had their milk delivered in those days, whatever the weather was like. Everything just carried on regardless. People carried on with their jobs, and I still went to school every day.

School hardly ever closed, but if it did, I found out too late. There wasn't the ability to communicate like there is today. The only way for me to find out if school had shut was if I went there in person. Most of the teachers lived near to the school so if enough of them managed to make the journey into school, it was open. But if the heating system broke down and the school was too cold, it was closed. The school keeper nearly always got the heating system working again, though. If we couldn't stay at school, I had a hard journey home, battling through the elements. The snow and wind together managed to sap out every bit of warmth that had been trapped inside my coat. By the time I got to school, I was already cold and wet. My shoes had become soaked and no longer protected my feet from the cold. The return home felt even harder to endure. And even though I took the same route home, somehow that return journey seemed even longer. I rarely met up with any of my friends outside when it was like that. That shows how much I preferred being at school, rather than staying at home.

During school lunchtime, a group of us often liked to go together to the Thames. St Mary's Church is next to a pathway that goes to the Thames foreshore. Opposite the church on the left side, there used to be a white building called The Old Swan Restaurant. We walked along the wall of the riverside restaurant. It had big windows overlooking the river. When the tide was out, we could walk along the foreshore and have a bit of fun. Us boys knew how to get up to mischief and liked to light a fire made out of driftwood. We then looked for discarded aerosol cans, which were in abundance, and threw them directly into the hot fire. We had to make a run for it because the cans exploded with a loud bang when they heated up. Sometimes, the blast expelled bits of glowing ember out of the fire which went everywhere! It was great fun, and we went to the riverside to do this many times.

The London Battersea Helicopter helipad was little bit further upriver. People were able to get quite close to the helipad and stand there to watch the helicopters take off. So close that the roar of the engines could be heard and the power force of the helicopter's blades rotating and pushing the air. A lot of business people used the helicopter as a fast mode of transport into the city, before getting into a waiting car to continue their journey. I wouldn't have liked to live close to the helipad because of the amount of noise that the helicopters generated both day and night.

If there happened to be a fire drill at Sinjun's, the entire school had to stand in the playground where we were all ordered to stand in our house groups. There were other rare occasions where we were ordered to the playground, like when a fight had broken out between boys at our school and a neighbouring school. I can recall one such occasion when both the lower and the upper school were made to stand in the playground at the same time. The headmaster, JJ O'Brien, was not at all amused. He did not like or appreciate his pupils bringing any kind of bad reputation to his school. There was a Royal Academy of Dancing next to Sinjun's School. It had a massive window that went the entire length of a room that overlooked our playground. There were mirrors on both sides of the room and a handrail for the dancers to use whilst doing their routines. Our punishment was to have to stand and watch the girls doing their dance routines. We were made to keep our hands firmly behind our backs and stand with good posture. No talking was permitted. But as far as punishments went, it wasn't that bad because I liked facing the window of the dancing academy.

I can vividly remember a time when I was in the playground playing football with some of my friends. One of the boys announced that he had figured out a way to get a lot closer to the window of the dancing academy. The wall on the side of the building was three metres high. Besides that, there was a glass roof with a walkway underneath it, and next to that, there was the main wall of the dance room. Without any warning, the boy kicked his football up and onto the glass roof. He thought that it was a clever plan because he then had to go to retrieve the ball. It meant that he would be able to get a really good look, up close, through the window. We stood and watched with interest as he climbed over the wall and onto the glass roof. But the boy hadn't even got very far when the glass shattered loudly and he fell down onto the ground beneath him. It was quite a shock for us to watch. He hurt himself very badly. I don't think that anyone ever tried to copy him. And despite all of his efforts, the boy never got a good look into that room!

Happy Times

I visited my Great-aunt Ciss frequently at the weekend. If I went to see her on a Sunday, I stayed to enjoy a Sunday roast with her. We ate at her small kitchen table which was next to a large sash window. When the weather was nice, I carried her table outside into the garden so that we could enjoy our meal there. On a few of the weekends that I visited Aunt Ciss, we went to Brighton together to meet up with her brother, Tommy Frohock. He and his wife liked to go for a walk along Brighton Pier with us and maybe visit some of the shops there as well. On other occasions, we hired deckchairs and sat on the stony beach for the day. They were happy times. It was so good to see my own family, rather than spend time with David's family. Aunt Ciss also took me to Tommy's home for Sunday dinner. He was a master butcher and knew his trade very well. The meat that he brought home was always top quality. Once cooked, it was very tasty and melted in the mouth.

Aunt Ciss started to take me to visit other members of my family. Aunt Dolly was one of them. It was so good to see her again as the last time that I had that privilege had been when I was seven years old. We visited on a Sunday and all went to St Paul's and St Peter's Church. The morning service was carried out by my Uncle Laurence, who was the pastor. Aunt Dolly liked to make her own fruit jam, which she always had stored in the back of her cupboard. When it was time for us both to go home, Aunt Dolly gave us a few jars to take with us. Another relative that we visited was Arthur Jennings, his wife Winnie and their boys. Ciss was close friends with Arthur, and they always sent each other cards at Christmas. We never got to see Ted, Jean, Tony or Edward Martin. Aunt Ciss would only talk to me about how they were getting on, like how Ted and his son Edward were still going to Chelsea Football Club every week. They were both ardent football fans and had season tickets. Tony had moved abroad with his family, but he still remained in contact with Ciss by sending letters. They wrote regularly so that they could keep up with family affairs. We talked about the lives of other family members that either of us didn't see. Aunt Ciss often asked me about Grandad Charlie and whether I had been to see him. For a reason unknown to me, they had fallen out with each other, but they were still interested in how the other person was.

During the evening or at weekends, I sometimes went with some of my friends to an ice skating rink in Streatham. It wasn't very long after we started going there that the rink got shut down for major repairs. All of the regular skaters went to Richmond Ice Rink so that they could continue skating. It wasn't a very big inconvenience as it was easy to get there by bus. Due to its popularity, there was always a long queue to get inside, but it was worth the wait because my friends and I thought that it was great fun. I bought myself a decent second-hand pair of skates and went quite regularly.

My schoolfriend Dennis and I were really good friends out of school too. He lived in a house close to Southfield's Station, and quite often, he and the other boy used to ride their bikes to where I lived so that we could all go out cycling together. Eland Road and Glycena Road lead off of Lavender Hill next to Battersea Town Hall and they are both very steep. We liked to start at the top of Glycena Road at Lavender Hill and look down at the road sloping away in front of us. The thrill was to gain as much bike speed as possible from the top to the bottom. We all had racing bikes so they were pretty fast! Like many of our pastimes in those days, this brought a fair amount of risk of injury. As the speeding bikes got near to the bottom of the hill, we had to put the brakes on gently at first, slowing the wheels down gradually. If the brakes went on too forcefully, there was a risk of getting flung forward over the handlebars! Unfortunately, this is exactly what happened to Dennis. He rode down the hill with such speed that he must have misjudged his distance. He started to brake too late and had to break harder. Poor Dennis went straight over his handlebars and hit the ground face-first. I was not there that day, but I heard that Dennis had to be rushed to hospital so that he could have stitches because his teeth went through his lip.

Final Days

I had almost completed my education at Sinjun's and was studying even harder in preparation for my final exams. Even though the exams were a big deal, I felt very confident that I would do well due to my grades and the comments from the teachers that I had received so far. I felt optimistic that it was going to be a good year for me. I did a lot of sailing that year, and we went rain or shine. The weather never stopped us from going onto the lake. There were three pupils to a boat and I always managed to end up with the same sixth form boy who pointed his finger to me when it was time to get into the sailing boats.

The sixth former didn't call me by my name despite knowing it. In those days, it was common to call someone by their surname, only occasionally by the first name. He never called me by either of my names. Instead, he gave me the nickname 'Diver'. The boy had black hair, was quite stockily built and his nose looked as if it had been broken because it was flat in the middle. I must admit that he was great fun to be around and a good friend to be with. As soon as we were in the middle of the lake, he used to tip the boat right onto its side so that I and the other boy with us got drenched in the water, whilst he remained dry inside the boat! After a few lessons, I knew what was about to happen and I just dove straight in, hence the nickname Diver. He called me that whenever he saw me around school too. After that, we became very good friends.

I had reached the time where I was ready to take my school exams. Since my younger years, I had aspired to become a heating engineer and follow in my grandad's footsteps. I was doing very well in technical drawing and my tutor told me that I would make a good draftsman. I enjoyed drawing in general, and for a while, I was very tempted to go that way for an apprenticeship. However, I decided not to go down that path in the end. I suspected that my reading and spelling capability at the time might have let me down, even though it had greatly improved over the years. Instead, I decided to seek employment as a heating engineer. All of the businesses in the heating trade took on apprentices, and they were quite competitive with one another. Employee's pay was all at standard rates across the board, and it was set up by the unions. I took the initiative to write to all of the companies in the heating game that I could think of to seek an apprenticeship with them.

I got a good response and attended many interviews. As many as twenty boys turned up to the interviews at the bigger companies. We were all ushered into a room to sit the CITB Health, Safety and Environment test. It was a multiple choice test on health, safety and environmental issues in construction. However, CITB also had a premises in London where applicants could take their exam. That way, it was no longer necessary to do tests at every interview. The examiners never gave a percentage, only a pass or fail. So I went along and sat the test. There was a nerve-wrecking wait after the test was completed because participants were never told the outcome there and then. I had to wait for a letter in the post to find out. When the letter arrived a week later, I could not wait to open it and tore at the envelope in excited anticipation. I was happy to read that I had passed the test and that I would no longer be required to do tests at interviews.

I had considered becoming an engineer in Her Majesty's Royal Navy so I applied for a job. The Royal Navy's recruiting office was in Holborn. One of the things that drew me towards this career direction was what I had known about my Uncle Ernie's time in the services. I arrived for the interview in good time and noticed that there were a lot of other candidates there too. We were all ushered into a very large room with tables that had been set out in lines. There were four tables at the front of the room for the training officers who were conducting the interviews. We all sat the exam together, before being called to the front individually to be questioned. I was asked why I wanted to be in the Navy and about certain parts of the exam, especially the English section. I was to find out that I had failed that section due to my poor spelling ability. Because of this, I was unsuccessful in my application. I didn't feel overly disappointed about it as it was just an option and may have only been a last resort. I was still waiting to hear back from some of the companies that I had applied to so I was still feeling hopeful about my future.

It wasn't very long before I received a letter from a company called H Page & Sons Engineering. They had an office in the London Borough of Southwark, just off of Long Lane in Weston Street. I wanted to make a good impression so

I was grateful when my neighbour offered me a blue pinstripe suit that he no longer wanted. It was a little bit too big for me, but it didn't look too bad. I found the contracts manager, Pat Connolly, to be very pleasant. It was he who conducted my job interview. He was very easy to talk to, and I felt that we got along very well. It was a small business, and there was only one heating and ventilation apprentice working for them at the time. Pat must have been very pleased with how I conducted myself during the interview. He gave me the job on the day, and I became H Page & Sons Engineering's second apprentice. I was over the moon!

I went home in a really good mood, like I was walking on clouds. I felt as if I had been offered a new start in life and couldn't help dreaming about my future. As soon as I got in, I changed out of the oversized suit and into my everyday clothes. By this time, I had had enough of wearing other people's hand-me-downs. I wanted to detach myself from the things that made me feel miserable in my past. It hadn't been all bad though. There were some occasions where boxes would just appear at home – I didn't know where they came from. They contained clothing items such as leather jackets. Quality items. If I asked Mum about their origins, I was simply told that they had fallen 'off the back of a lorry'. But these instances were few and far between and the suit reminded me of the not-so-good times in my life. My neighbour told me that he didn't want the suit back and that I could do whatever I wanted with it. I took it to the big refuse bins that were at the bottom of the flats and took great delight in getting rid of it. I didn't just throw it away. I set it alight! It was cathartic watching that old suit burning because its destruction symbolised a kind of release. I made a pledge to myself that I would never wear other people's discarded clothing again.

Pat sent me a confirmation letter detailing my terms of employment and a start date. I was instructed to be ready for work and present myself at the office no later than eight o'clock. The start date was on Monday morning a fortnight after I finished school. By this time, I had already received all of my exam results. I had sat exams in eight different subjects and passed them all. I had higher marks in English than mathematics, and I admit that that shocked me a little bit because I found English to be the harder subject out of the two. I was really pleased with myself. I told Mum the good news, but she didn't reveal any kind of emotion about it. I hadn't expected any kind of praise or recognition for my hard work as I never received any in the past.

My last day at school started off like any other school day. In my head, I was thinking that everything I was doing was for the last time. A lot of the boys wrote their names on each other's shirts. I kept my blazer on all day to prevent anyone from signing mine. After school had finished, some of the boys went to the pub with one or two of the teachers. I walked home alone and contemplated how my life was about to change, from being at school every day to going to work. I found out many years later that Sinjun's closed in 1986 and that the school building closed a couple of years later in 1988. I felt very nervous about my future as everything from then on would be completely new to me. My apprenticeship would take two years pipe fitting City & Guilds, one year of gas pipe fitting City & Guilds and one year arc welding pipe City & Guilds. I learned that I would be on block release. That meant that I would be at college weeks at a time, rather than attending one day a week.

I was booked in for four years' study at Tottenham College of Technology doing block release. I bought myself a bib and brace, overalls and a pair of steel toecap boots from Jay's Supplies in Lavender Hill for my first day on a building site. In those days, it wasn't a requirement to wear hard hats or high visibility clothing. If you were lucky, the company that you worked for might have issued a donkey jacket. I didn't need to take tools with me, I just needed a tape measure and a seven-inch spirit level that I bought from a tool shop. I was sent to one of the sites in the heart of the City of London. The site belonged to the Bank of Spain in London Wall, Moorgate. I was very nervous and excited at the same time. It was Sunday, the day before my first day in my new job. I wanted to make sure that I could find the place okay and didn't want to be late. I mapped the entire journey out and then travelled it to see how long it would take to get there. By doing these things, I felt ready for my new start in life.

Coming of Age

When I arrived at work on Monday morning, I met the foreman and a couple of pipe fitters who also worked for H Page & Sons Engineering. The work on the bank had only just started compared to other sites. It was quite a small building with four floors and a basement. The building was very old and in urgent need of new pipework and modernisation. A whole new heat system was being installed. We worked in the morning, then when it came to lunchtime, everyone ventured off-site to the local pub. All of the pubs were packed solid with office workers and builders like myself. I had been introduced to the pub culture. How anyone did any work in the afternoons beats me. Builders returned to the site and played cards for money. To me, it was a great life. If anyone got too drunk, they found a place to sleep it off. Most days were like this.

My first week was coming to an end, which was of course a Friday. It was payday, and I received my cash wages in a small brown envelope. We never had it paid into our bank accounts. On one side of the envelope had my name on it and the other side had wage amount with the tax and National Insurance that had been deducted. One of the fitters took it upon himself to go to the office and collect all of the envelopes, then deliver them to everyone else on-site. People didn't like carrying too much money in case they lost it or someone tried to steal it from them. My first pay packet was to the value of £28.50. It was not a lot, but it was a start. I still kept my job in the cafe to top my weekly money up.

My friends told me about a club that they had started to go to on Friday or Saturday nights. It was called Cheekee Pete's and was situated right next to the river at Richmond-upon-Thames. The club was well known for its two floors with a different sound system playing in each; one playing old town and the other soul music. The club was always packed solid with people who were around the same age as me. Despite this, there was never any kind of trouble, either inside or outside the club. Everyone was mainly interested in having a good time on the dance floors. There was a stairwell that went up in the middle of the building. Both floors had a lobby area with a drinks bar adjacent to the lobby. Here, people could go to mingle and have a chat away from the loud music. Everyone that went there was there for a good time. It was a great place to meet new friends too. Up to this point, my dancing skills had been a bit poor. I was very stiff, but I soon learned to dance by watching and copying my friends. I started to get great enjoyment out of dancing and often stayed out with my friends all night. It was actually quite exhausting at times, but I found it to be good exercise, like carrying out training. It helped me with my fitness for when I played rugby.

On one occasion while I was dancing at Cheekee Pete's, I took a shine to a girl who was a year older than myself. She had beautiful, blonde hair that was very wavy. We got talking one time and hit it off almost straightaway. She told me that her name was Nicola and that she lived in Sunbury-on-Thames. She must have taken a shine to me too because she gave me her phone number before the night was over. I couldn't give her my phone number in return as Mum and David didn't have a phone at home, but there was a red phone box in close proximity to the flats that we lived in. Red phone boxes accepted two pence and ten pence coins, and I would sometimes be talking with the girl for hours so I had to make sure that I had plenty of change on me. It was not very long before Nicola asked me to come to her house and meet her family. She asked me to have Sunday dinner with them, and I happily accepted the invitation. I rode my bike to Clapham Junction Railway Station and then put it in the parcel carriage because bikes were not permitted on the passenger carriages. That's where bikes went in those days.

When I got off of the train at my destination, Nicola was already standing there waiting for me. We walked and talked together down The Avenue. As we were walking down, she stopped and pointed between two houses towards a well-known rugby club, London Irish, then we continued to walk to her house. We talked the whole way there. I was given a very warm welcome as soon as I had stepped inside the front door. Nicola's mother had almost finished preparing dinner so we went straight into the dining room. The family had a six-seater dining table, quite similar to Grandad Charlie's. The table had already been laid out with cutlery, glasses and China plates.

We were encouraged to take our places at the table whilst Nicola and her mum brought the food in and arranged it down the middle of the table. It was quite a spectacular display, and I felt very honoured to be there. We all got along very well, and the conversation flowed so easily. The subject of sport came up and lead onto rugby. Nicola's brother was a year younger than me, and I found out that he was also a keen rugby player who played on Sundays for a local club. Both he and the father enjoyed going to the club as they were massive supporters of the game. The father liked to watch his son playing as often as he was able to. It only took about three weeks from our introduction before I was asked by Nicola's brother to play for his side on Sundays.

The club was called Universal Vandales Rugby Club, and I agreed to play alongside the girl's brother for their youth team. The club was in Walton-upon-Thames, not far from their house so we took our bikes and rode there before the game was due to start. I played in the backs during that first game and enjoyed it so much that I continued to play in that team for the whole season. The main teams played on Saturday afternoons. It was a very well organised and set up club as the boys played in their years. At the time, the club had a small bar and social area. We often went with the dad to the bar after the games where he would buy us a Coke each. The club had its regular supporters who either lived locally or came to watch the kids play. There was one lady who really stood out to me. She was wearing green wellington boots and a green wax jacket. She looked like a farmer's wife, but she really acted in a British '70s' sitcom called The Good Life and was a very well-known actress at the time. Her name was Sue Perkins, and she liked to drink a pint of beer next to the bar. Sue was pleasant to be around and liked to engage in good conversation with everyone. She came out with things that were funny and had a great personality. Everybody liked her.

I was visiting or meeting up with Nicola most weekends by this time. I even took her to meet Aunt Ciss. I felt that her approval was important to me as she was more of a mother to me than my own mum. Sometimes, I went with Nicola and her family to the cinema and sometimes we were all treated to a meal out, which Nicola's dad paid for. I always felt very privileged to be invited to enjoy those times with the family. We both went out on our bikes often and sometimes travelled miles just to go to a park. One time, we even drove our bikes all the way to visit my grandad and Hilda, which they were very happily surprised by.

When I visited Grandad and Hilda, I always made a point of turning up unannounced. I had a good reason for not letting him know that I was coming. I

133

was told to phone first, and it felt to me like I was being asked to make an appointment. He never liked anyone turning up out of the blue, and when I unexpectedly turned up, Grandad had a moan at Mum about it. I also made a point of not dressing smart because I knew that Grandad didn't like it. But even though I got the feeling that my appearance really bothered him, he never did anything about the fact that his grandson was growing up looking like a tramp. Nevertheless, he always seemed pleased to see me. Nicola and I spent the afternoon there, and when it was time to go home, Hilda encouraged Grandad to take us back in the car so that we didn't have to cycle home. Grandad put our bikes in the back of the car and took us both with him.

One weekend, I turned up at her parent's house unexpectedly. I didn't know that the family had made plans to go away on holiday. They owned a caravan which was parked on the drive. Nicola's dad told me that I would not be able to stay that weekend due to them going away. I spent the day with Nicola and left in the evening to get the train home from Sunbury Station. I hadn't brought my bike on that occasion and regretted it when I had to run the length of The Avenue, which was exactly a mile long. I missed it. I had no way of getting home that evening or telling Mum and David that I was stranded in Sunbury. It was very late so I walked back to Nicola's house and threw pebbles at her bedroom window to get her attention. She didn't want to let her parents know that I was outside because she had been told that I was not allowed to stay that night. Nicola threw a sleeping bag and a pillow down to me. I crawled underneath the caravan and settled down for the night until the birds starting chirping. I got back to London on the milk train in the morning. Nicola and I continued to go out together for almost a year before our relationship ended.

The owner of the cafe liked me a lot. He offered me an apprenticeship as a chef, but I turned the offer down because I preferred working in the heating profession. I found it to be very interesting and the day went quicker than it did when I was working in the cafe. He seemed very disappointed when I told him that I didn't want to be a chef, but I think that he understood. There was a small telly high up on a shelf in the corner of the cafe. It was there for people to watch whilst they ate. On Saturdays, we put sports on like football, horse racing and rugby. I used to love to watch the rugby and couldn't wait until I could play on Saturdays for a team. But at the time, I was still playing for Universal Vandals on Sundays. I had a full week of things to keep my life busy. I kept on working at the cafe until I was earning sufficient money in my heating engineer job. I left about a year later, but I remained good friends with Michael and often went into the cafe after I finished work for a cup of tea with him.

Rugby Netball

Mr TI Jones approached my friend Dennis, another boy and I to ask if we wanted to play rugby netball for his team. The club that he played for had evening matches at Clapham Common once or twice a week during the summertime. We felt quite honoured and, of course, we said yes. All three of us were hungry for the game, both rugby union and rugby netball. We arrived together at Clapham Common at about 6:30 PM and met the rest of the team at the changing rooms. There was a bandstand as well as a cafeteria near to the changing rooms. There were small square tables with chessboards built into the top of them outside the cafeteria. People had been playing chess and draughts on Clapham Common since 1920 and were able to take part most evenings. I loved to get up there early just to watch the chess matches and to hopefully improve my own game. At the time, rugby netball was highly popular. There were just two leagues when my friends and I started playing. However, I was told that there had been up to four leagues in previous years. But people didn't only play rugby netball in league matches. Almost every part of the common had rugby netball games being played, apart from a few rugby league games and Gaelic football.

Once the groundsmen opened the wooden gate to the changing rooms, I and the other players filed in. They were wooden huts with a drinking water trough outside that had cold water taps hung above it. There were lots of changing rooms and each had wooden benches that went the full length of both sides. Once we were changed, we made our way to the pitches. Each team took responsibility for carrying a post and a net to the pitch. Then once they were erected at each end, we were ready to start the game. Watching the games had been exciting but, now that I was actually about to play the game myself, I could really feel the adrenaline pumping. Most of my team members were strangers to me. I only knew my friends from school and TI Jones, who had played for Old Town for quite some time.

The rules of rugby netball were just like football except kicking was not allowed. It was a lot different to playing rugby union as we were throwing the ball forwards to get it up the pitch and closer to the net. Tackling in rugby netball was on a one-to-one basis. There were no scrums either. Instead, a player from each team stood opposite each other and the referee bounced the ball between them. It was down to them to compete for possession. On this particular evening, the weather was dry and hot, and due to the recent run of good weather, the ground was very hard. The tackles were hard too, especially when tackled to the floor.

It was tiring playing during the summer months as the air was humid and we were constantly running back and forward, tackling the opposition for control of the ball. This game was a lot faster than rugby union, and it required a lot of stamina. On the way back to the changing rooms, most of the players used the water trough to drink the cold tap water and douse themselves in it.

It was very refreshing and cooling. After we were changed, some of us went to the pub. It was called The Windmill and was situated on the south side of the common. I went home that evening buzzing from my experience. The next day, I awoke and felt so stiff that I could just about walk. When I examined my body, I noticed that I had quite a few bruises over my body and a slightly blackened eye. I wasn't put off by it though. I found it to be a good way of letting go of aggression, which was great because I felt like I had a lot of inner aggression to offload at that time. My friends and I had a great time playing, and we couldn't wait to play again.

There was one particular evening when I arrived early to watch the men playing chess next to the changing rooms. As I was wandering between the small chess tables, I came across a man who was sitting alone. I recognised him instantly as the man who has accompanied me whilst running up Lavender Hill and all of the way around Clapham Common. He gave me a broad grin and then asked me if I would be interested in playing a game with him. I told him that I didn't have long before the rugby netball match started, to which he replied, "Better make it a quick one then." I agreed and sat down opposite him.

The man beat me at the chess game. We didn't speak very much during our game, but something that we did discuss was my running. The man asked me how it was going, and I told him that I was doing really well as I had become much stronger since our last encounter. But I noticed that he raised his right hand to his face whilst in deep thought, just like me. We did it at the same time and I thought that that was funny. There was something really familiar about the man's face. Not only because we had already met before whilst running, it was because of something else, but I couldn't quite put my finger on it. I felt comfortable in the man's company, like I'd known him all of my life. He spoke to me with a very soft voice and had a good way of communicating, especially when he explained to me how he had won the chess game. He told me that if I could plan three, or even five moves, in my head I'd always be in front of the other player. As I got up from the chair, he said, "Good luck." I thanked the man for the game, and we shook hands before I went on to the changing rooms.

Suburbia

Mum applied for a housing transfer to Southfields. She was successful in her application, and we moved to a block of flats on an estate in Fernwood, Albert Drive. It was a three-bedroom flat near Wimbledon tennis courts and not very far from Southfields Train Station. It was our first home with central heating; it came from the boiler house on the estate. The flat was well laid out with a toilet room and bathroom on the right near to the front door, then my bedroom on the left side. There was a huge cast iron radiator on the same wall as my bedroom and another in the living room. None of the three bedrooms had heating. When the weather was really cold, I left my bedroom door open so that the heat from the hallway could come in. The next room along from mine belonged to my two sisters, then the last one was Mum and David's. The living room and kitchen were opposite.

The flat was on the left side of the building on the second floor. We lived on the top of a hill and the panoramic views from the front room window and the balcony were astounding. We still didn't have the luxury of a home phone. If we needed to make a call, we had to use one of the two red public phone boxes at the end of our block. I had to make new friends all over again, but it didn't take me very long as we lived on quite a big estate. I was already good friends with some of the boys because they went to Sinjun's. I thought that Southfields was a very nice place to live. The teenagers there were really friendly. Once I met one, I met everyone else really easily.

Rugby Union

When the rugby netball season had come to an end and rugby union was starting up, TI Jones asked whether Dennis and I would be interested in playing for his club, Merton RFC. It had not been very long since I finished playing for University Vandals and I was looking for another club to play for. TI Jones' proposal was ideal. Dennis' friend came along too. We did some training before play commenced. Training held at their club fields on a Wednesday evening. The three of us were put into their senior sides, and we played for the veterans and third team. Really, I wanted to play for a Colts team with boys my own age. However, Merton didn't have one at the time. They were talking about having one soon. I knew that Hammersmith and Fulham RFC were about to start a Colts team.

Hurlingham Park is the home for Hammersmith & Fulham Rugby Club. I got to know quite a few players due to playing against them in rugby netball, and once or twice, I played for Merton RFC. Hammersmith & Fulham club members met in a school gym and playground once a week for training. I was happy about this because I didn't have to go very far from home. As part of our training, we went out together for long runs. We normally ran from the school, over Putney Bridge and then back to the school again. They were pretty intense training sessions, but they were good.

The club was organising a Colts under 21 team. I played in the first Hammersmith & Fulham Colts game as hooker. I didn't get on very well and was unable to win much ball in the scrum. I was still learning that position and the communication between myself and our scrum half poor. Just as they started up their Colts side, Merton were seeking under 21s to play for them. Ken Phillips was the man to organise it, and he put a lot of his time and effort in to make it work. A few other members also helped him. I continued to play for the Colts until I was twenty-one, then their thirds and second teams. Dennis had already decided after a few games that he was going to play for London

Irish and this was to be the last game that he played alongside me. Unlike Dennis, I felt at home when I was at Merton and stayed for many years to come.

Whilst playing as a Colt for Merton I attended a dinner night that was laid on especially for the Colts team. Tables had been put out around the club room and they had baskets on them that were filled with sliced French bread. They had really made an effort. It wasn't very long after we had sat down before someone decided to throw a piece of the bread at someone. After that, the air was full of bread pieces going in all directions! I don't think that much of it actually got eaten, but nobody went hungry. The meal went down really well. After we had finished eating and had drunk a few beers, two of the tables got pushed together in preparation for a game. Three chairs were placed on opposite sides of the tables, then six pint-sized beer glasses were placed in front of each of the six people that agreed to take part. Nobody knew what they were letting themselves in for.

They were playing a game called Rabbits. Someone brought a full jug of beer over and placed it in the centre of the table. One of the senior players at the club was an organiser that night, and he stood at one end of the table. For the purpose of the game, he was known as the chairman. He was the one who did all of the talking, as well as dishing out any punishment that he saw fit. He then proceeded to explain the game rules to us all, in quite a formal tone. It made the game seem so much more exciting, as if it was in some kind of courtroom. To start off play, the chairman pointed towards one of the six people that were sat at the table. He called out 'Rabbits!' and held his hands up beside his head to represent rabbit ears, waving them backwards and forwards. The players on each side of him had to hold up just one hand and wave it backwards and forwards. That hand was the one closest to the player that the chairman had pointed to in the first instance. It was then the first player's turn to point at a player on the opposite side of the table. The game carried on, to and fro, until someone got it wrong. It was then down to the chairman to decide how much he, or the rest of his team, had to drink. Either a full pint or half a pint of beer. It didn't take very long for someone to leave the table to go to the little boy's room. It was at the end of the changing rooms, then another and then another. Those who left the table were all replaced with fresh candidates until everyone had had a go. The dinner night went on until very late and I had no chance of making it home. There were a few others in the same situation so we stayed at one of the other boy's house.

I had now turned twenty year's old and playing for Merton Colts Under 21s. I had started to play sevens in the summer months, too. I was still playing rugby netball in the evening. I notice now, that for some reason that year, I became very physical on the pitch. I got pulled up quite frequently by whoever was refereeing the game. One referee marched me away, quite far from the pitch, so that nobody else would be able to hear him shout at me. I knew that all I could respond with was 'yes, sir', 'no, sir'. We didn't get issued cards back then. Players always had subs so players just got told off for most things that happened on the pitch. Then they got a ban for four weeks.

It was coming to the end of the season, and we had four games left. I was playing in the pack during one of those final games, and it was almost half time. Our centre back was an average-sized boy, and he was having trouble with the centre on the opposing side. He was very big and broad, almost twice the size at 6 ft 2. He was playing dirty too. Instead of pushing players away with an open hand, he closed it into a fist and then pushed his opponent, knocking him to the floor. Our centre back was no match for him. He came to me after a short time playing and told me what was happening. I suggested that he swap positions with me. I was bigger and more of a challenge.

As they came out of the scrum, I saw that they had possession of the ball, and I watched it make its way to their centre back. He came towards me holding the ball and put out his hand to push me off. I ducked low down and came up again with my shoulder against his body. I lifted him right up into the air and his feet left the ground. He fell hard onto the floor. I should have stopped there, but I didn't. I followed it through with a fist to the side of his head. The player was out cold. The referee saw what had happened and stopped the game. It was abandoned, and I was banned from taking part in any other games for four weeks. That meant that I was not able to finish the season.

I started running harder, getting ready for the rugby netball season. I started to run from Fulham along Minster Road, then down New King's Road, up to Wandsworth Bridge Road, across the bridge, turn right into Swandon Way. Then Putney Bridge Road and over Putney Bridge, back down New King's Road and back home again. My first game was played against Battersea Ironside. There was a guy on their team that always seemed to want to tackle me. On one particular tackle in the game, he took me to the ground. As I turned my head to the left, I could see the ball rolling away from us. He still had to hold me, and he had gotten right on top of me. We were face to face. I thought that he would use that situation to really hurt me so I didn't give him the opportunity. I pulled at his shirt, bringing him closer to me, then punched him several times in the face before throwing him to the side of me. He didn't get up. He was out cold.

I had reached another pivotal moment in my life. I recognised that I was getting out of control on and off of the pitch. The problem was that I had started to enjoy inflicting pain. Deep down in my mind, I knew that I would eventually go too far and hurt someone really badly. The recent experience really shook me, and I made a promise to myself to stop the violent acts. If I ended up in a confrontation, I'd talk my way out of it or simply walk away. Being disallowed from taking part in the sport that I loved really hurt me. I didn't enjoy watching the sports that I was involved in as much as I did taking part. I got quite upset when I couldn't play.

Independence

The sport that I was playing had really changed my body shape. I had been quite small in the past and very slim. But I had become much taller, broader and more muscle defined. I was transformed from a boy into a man and was at the age where I was taking a keen interest in girls. One particular girl really caught my attention when I was on a night out with a friend at Micawber's Wine Bar. Her name was Cathy Cosgrove and she had travelled from Fulham to enjoy a night out with her friends. We instantly struck a chord with one another and talked a lot as the night went on. We discovered that we had a common interest in our love of sport.

Cathy had been into swimming for a lot of her younger days and had only recently stopped, just a year before our first encounter. Cathy had been part of the Great Britain swimming team that competed in the 1980 Summer Olympics in Moscow, Russia. She explained to me how she had trained extremely hard in a gruelling regime to get there. Before the main event, she was required to do a qualifying swim which involved touching pads to record the time. Unfortunately, Cathy didn't touch the pads hard enough, which meant that her time was not recorded and she was unable to swim in the main event. Sharron Davies won a silver medal in the women's 400-metre individual medley event. However, there was some controversy surrounding the outcome as the gold medal winner, Petra Schneider, admitted later on that she had been aided by the use of steroids as part of the East German state-run doping programme. Sharron went on to be recognised as a great swimmer and received an MBE for services to swimming. Cathy didn't compete at such a high level again.

Cathy and I had been together for almost a year when I turned eighteen years of age. During that year, I spent a lot more of my social time in Fulham. Cathy lived in Munster Road, and she was very good friends with Sam and Graham who lived at number ten, opposite Cathy's family home. Sam and Graham's mother spent most of the time living abroad in South Africa. Cathy's friends were at home alone a lot so Cathy and I used to stay at their house at weekends and sometimes during the week. We all got along really well as we were a similar age. Their mother had given up her contract agreement with the landlord so they started a new one for themselves.

The landlord used the opportunity to raise the rent so that it was in line with other rent costs at that time. It was a fair amount more than Sam and Graham's mother had been paying. They had to seek another person to share the house bills if they wanted to remain in the home that they had grown up in. I never thought that that person would be me; however, I was eagerly offered the tempting opportunity to move in with them. I thought about their offer seriously and decided that I didn't want to stay with Mum and David any more. I made my mind up to move out. There was nothing to stop me as I was at an age where I could leave home if I wanted to. The house had three bedrooms, a large living room, a kitchen and two bathrooms. The ground floor was rented by an elderly woman who had lived in the house for years and would remain there until her death.

At this time, Mum had a telephone installed at home. I phoned her up if I needed to let her know that I was going to stay out. There was one occasion that David picked the phone up. He told me that I was not allowed to stay out and that I had to be back home at a certain time. To avoid an argument, I told David that I would be home shortly. When I arrived home, I told Mum that I had decided to move out and that I was leaving that evening. Mum was really upset about my announcement and she started to cry. She asked me to stay but I had made up my mind that it was my time to leave. David was at home, but he didn't intervene. He stayed in the front room and didn't make any effort to stop me from leaving. I quickly got some clothes and my shoes together without wasting any time. I walked out of the door with no regrets and was happy that I had the full freedom to do whatever I chose to do without asking for permission. Even though my mother had been very upset about my leaving at first, she soon came around to it. I still visited her as much as I wanted to. My bedroom was still there for me for when I wanted to stay over, or maybe come back again if things went wrong. We both knew that I had nowhere else to go.

Cathy made the decision to leave her parent's home and move into Sam and Graham's house with me. Cathy's parents didn't mind because she had not gone far and they would still be able to see her whenever they wanted to. None of us earned very much money. Even though there were now four of us paying the rent, we were still finding it hard to make ends meet so we took in more lodgers. I was not used to sharing my living space with complete strangers. But it was something that I had to do if I wanted to have money left over for leisure time. We were out every weekend! The majority of my money was spent on going out. I saved just enough to pay for work travel. Some weekends, Merton Rugby Club held functions. I liked to go along to them. The clubhouse was packed with a lot of the players congregating around the bar. Someone always started singing rugby songs and everyone joined in. The atmosphere was great and they were really good nights. I was still cycling to get to places and used to ride to Parsons Green, put my bike on the train, get off at the end of the Northern Line Underground station at Morden then ride up to the club. I did the same journey in reverse to get home again, which was a bit difficult after a few pints of beer.

College Life

The first two years of my apprenticeship studying Heating Ventilation (pipe fitting) had come to an end. I sat my City & Guilds examination, which I found to be very difficult, I was sitting in the college canteen with one of my friends when another student from the class came over to us with the news about the exam results. Two students had passed and I was relieved to find out that I was one of them. I felt extremely proud of myself and was shocked that only two of us had passed. The rest of the class had to resit the parts of the exam that they had failed on. During the next two years, I learned to become a gas pipework welder.

I was in the second year at college when a basketball tournament was held between the different departments. I was asked to play with the welding department which was in the year above me. Our team played really well on that day considering the fact that we had never played as a team before. I managed to score a few baskets and we went on to win the tournament. The tutor who organised different sports in the college approached me and asked if I would be interested in playing for the college. I gladly accepted his offer. The matches were held after the college day had ended. The tutor kept me as a sub, and I only got to play part of the game. He did this on several occasions. I got fed up because I really wanted to play a full game so I stopped going to the matches.

The tutor also played a lot of rugby. He was quite a stocky man which was a typical build for a rugby player. He played for Harlequins, which was one of the top rugby clubs at the time. During my last year of study, the tutor got together a rugby team to represent the college, and he asked me if I wanted to play. I keenly accepted his offer. I had to take an afternoon off of work because I was not learning at college that particular week. We played against a college that had a reputation for being very good and well drilled. I played 'hooker' for that game. The tutor played in it too. It was a challenging game, but I really enjoyed it. Both sides played very hard, and it was very close, right to the end when the final whistle was blown. We won, just. The score, 13 to 12, reflected each player's efforts. To us, it was a great game, and we felt victorious.

When the year was finished, I received very high marks in the practicals that had taken place in the workshop. I also passed the gas welding City & Guilds exam. I was happy to get very high marks in the practical exam for arc welding but was quite disappointed when I failed on a multiple question paper. Our new contract manager wouldn't let me resit it so I never got a certificate for arc welding City & Guilds. My Aunt Ciss had generously helped me to pay for my driving lessons in the previous year. I failed the first two driving test attempts, but it didn't put me off from trying again. I changed my driving instructor because I felt that the one I had was not very good. My new instructor helped me build up my confidence, then when I attempted the test for the third time, I was successful. My first car was a blue Ford Escort. Having a car meant that I could get to jobs a lot easier.

Cathy became pregnant in 1983 when I was nineteen years of age. It was a warm evening in late summer when Cathy told me that I was to become a father. It was dusk, and we were together in Bishop's Park, Fulham. We were sitting on a bench in front of the Thames with Putney Bridge in view. I distinctly remember that Cathy was wearing bib and brace dungarees with a yellow t-shirt. I knew that she had something important to tell me, but it was still a big shock when the words came out of her mouth. We were both very young and always out enjoying our youth to the full. Even though I was living an adult life, I didn't feel as if I was adult enough to have the responsibilities of fatherhood. But we decided that we would give it a go. Cathy's parents were literally across the road and she had a caring extended family. Cathy and I had the house to ourselves because everyone else had moved out so there was room for us to start a family together. We were delighted to have a son in January 1984. We named him Laurence.

I liked to spend most of my social time drinking with friends in pubs in Fulham and Putney. Sometimes, we went down to the King's Road in Chelsea. After our drinking sessions, we usually ended up in a restaurant in Fulham Road. It was a very popular place for the locals. We carried on drinking there because it had a bar too. It was a short walk home from the restaurant, but there were quite a few occasions where I took my car. My friends and I went to several pubs so I always left the car at one of the first pubs. I was too intoxicated to drive home. By the next morning, I couldn't remember which pub I had left it at. When I woke up, I would walk around to all of the pubs, retracing my steps to find it, wasting half a day.

There was a group of us who went to George Best's club near Green Park Station. One of my friends who was with me knew George well. It was quite a big bar, and I used to see George sitting on his own at the end of the bar having a quiet drink. He never looked as if he wanted any company as he never engaged with anyone else. He just sat there. Nobody danced in the bar. They just sat or stood around talking. It had a pub atmosphere, but it was more refined. George and I never spoke to one another at the bar, but we did have an encounter several years later.

I was a welder at the time and was working in the lounge area of the LBC Radio Studios in Hammersmith. Gary Lineker was there that evening with his first wife, and we spoke briefly. He seemed to be a pleasant man. When George came into the building, he was right next to me, but I didn't speak to him. He was heavily intoxicated and slurring his words. He didn't look like he knew what he was doing! I laughed when I read my newspaper at work the next day and saw the story about George's interview at LBC Radio Studios. I told my work colleagues about what I had witnessed that night, and we all had a little laugh about it.

I enjoyed a good drink myself. On a hot summer's evening, I had just finished playing rugby netball. My good friend Michael, who was on the same side as me at Merton, asked me if I fancied doing a pub crawl back to mine. I accepted his offer. We did quite a few of the Young's pubs in Wandsworth. The last one was a Ferguson pub next to Chelsea Harbour. By this time, we had consumed quite a lot of alcohol, but that wasn't going to stop us from drinking even more.

I absolutely loved a good curry, I still do. There was a curry house on Stamford Bridge, and we decided to go there as I had used it before. We went inside and noticed that it was packed solid except for one table. Michael and I sat down and ordered lots of food. But I had only taken one mouthful when I suddenly and unexpectedly came over all funny. The whole room had started to move. With that, I got up and started to walk around the restaurant. Michael could see that I was in a bad way so he hastily paid the bill, and we both left. Once we were both outside, Michael flagged down a black taxi. We got in and were sitting on the back seat. I can't remember why but I was wearing

149

Michael's jacket at the time. I was feeling evermore sickly and the motion of the taxi moving wasn't helping. Sick came up into my mouth and, even though I did my best to hold it in, it started to trickle down my chin. I was trying not to get the sick on Michael's jacket, but it was too late. Sick spewed out of my gob with great force and onto the window that separated us and the cab driver. Michael's jacket was covered.

We had just turned the corner into Munster Road and pulled up outside my house. I got out and rang the doorbell. Cathy came to the small balcony above me and looked down. She could see that I was in no fit state to explain myself. Michael did it for me. I went up the stairs to the front room. Cathy took a bucket and sponges down to the cab and spent an hour cleaning it out. The cabbie was grateful for that. I slept upright on the sofa that night. I couldn't lay down or walk about. It was clear to see that I had alcohol poisoning and should have gone to the hospital that evening. I was still in bits the following day. It was at least three months before I could even look at another alcoholic drink. Being that drunk was quite a frightening experience. It had changed my views on alcohol consumption. A few years later, I went teetotal and stayed that way for many years after.

Every Christmastime, the work dwindled and H Page always ended up laying fitters and welders off. I was called into the office to see the contract manager. I entered his room where I met him sitting at his desk with a sheet of paper in front of him. There was a list of names on it, and I noticed that my name was at the very top. The contract manager told me that he had to let me go. That was the first time that I was made redundant. It was a common occurrence in the building trade at the time. But there was always a lot of work around so people were not unemployed for very long.

Enjoying Life

It had been a while since I had moved out and having the time and space to myself helped me to put the things that David had done in the past behind me. I saw him every now and then on-site as we both worked for the same building company based in Wimbledon. He was trying hard to be my friend.

House prices had started to rise everywhere and the company took advantage of the situation by buying houses and splitting them into flats. The plumber that was contracted to the company was overwhelmed, and he was desperate to find someone to help him with the work.

Bob took me on and I started by working together with him at first. I had never done any plumbing before and had only ever worked in the commercial sector. Bob and I did everything; heating systems, bathroom suites and drainage. The houses were empty and that made it easy to carry out the work. After a little while, Bob left me to get on with my work alone. He had taught me a lot about domestic plumbing and heating. One day, I carried out a job and didn't do a pipe joint properly. Water leaked out of the joint all night, but fortunately, there was no damage. Bob wanted to stop money out of my wage for the mistake. I couldn't believe the cheek. He had made a considerable amount of money out of me over the months that I had worked for him. We fell out over it and never worked together again.

I got more injuries from playing rugby netball than I did from playing rugby union. On one occasion, I took an awkward tackle against a player on the opposing team and sustained a broken ankle. I had to stay off of work for six weeks because I had to have a small plate fitted to heal the fracture. The hospital doctor told me not to take part in any sports until the plate had done its job and was removed. I would have to leave the plate in for two years. I couldn't wait to get back out there though. As soon as I was road running, I started the rugby back up again. I went against the advice that I was given by the doctor but playing rugby meant more to me than the plate in my ankle did and I was willing to take on the risk.

I always wanted to play in the forward pack. I had started off as wing forward and increased my weight from eleven stones at sixteen years of age up to sixteen and a half stones by the age of twenty-three. I gained the weight so that I could play prop forward. In my opinion, Merton had – and still has – the best social society where everyone gets along. I made many great memories there. I also played in the back row for Hammersmith and Fulham's third team from time to time. They enjoyed meeting up in the Peterborough Arm's pub in New Kings Road, Fulham. They held their meetings there as they didn't have the luxury of a clubhouse.

By this time, I was playing for Merton, and they put out two rugby netball teams to play in the summer. Their team was called Barflies, and I started to play for them instead of Old Town. I was a high scorer and scored in the majority of the games that I took part in. We won the second division in the first season that I played for them and moved straight up to the first division. From then on, the A team played first division games and the B team continued playing in the second division.

It was August 1985. I had accumulated a lot of knowledge in plumbing through my experiences and decided that I would run my own business. I started off by placing cards in shop windows, and it wasn't very long before I was busy with work and steadily building up my clientele. I was earning a lot of money and even had Mum over a couple of days a week to do my bookkeeping for me. She was quite happy to do so, and I paid her for helping me out. Life at the time was pretty good for me. I was doing very well with my business, as was Cathy who also had her own business. As the workload grew, I got involved with more contractors who were willing to pass on some of their workload. In a short space of time, I was able to provide employment for two other plumbers to assist me with my own workload.

I had a meeting arranged with a client for 10.30 in the morning. I had woken up feeling rough. My head felt as if someone was hitting me with a hammer, constant pounding. I had very little energy in me at all and felt very hot and sweaty. I just could not get up! Cathy was worried so she called her mother over to see if she could help. As soon as she looked at me, she could tell that I was unwell. I must have looked really ill because she went to the phone straightaway to order a local cab. Cathy's mother returned to my bedside and physically lifted me then helped me down three flights of stairs. By the time we got to the front door, the cab was there, ready. Cathy and her mother bundled me into the back seat, and we were then driven to St Stephen's Hospital (Chelsea and Westminster) in Fulham Road. The cab driver could see that I was ill so he drove us there as fast as he could. Cathy's mother already knew what was wrong with me, but she waited for the doctor to say it first. He took a short while examining me and said, "You have meningitis, Mr Jennings." I fell asleep.

When I woke up, I discovered that I had been moved to an isolation ward. I had my own private room so that I could be kept well away from the rest of the patients. After a discussion with a ward nurse, I discovered that I had been placed into the AIDS ward. It had been designed so that AIDS victims could come in 24 hours a day, every day, if they were ever feeling poorly and in need of professional care. Many came there to die. There was a lot of concern about the disease at that time because it was quite new. But I was not particularly worried about it, despite there being no known cure at the time. All of the nurses were male, which I thought was unusual. After a couple of days of bed rest, my health did not seem to be improving. The doctors ran a few more tests, which showed that I had pneumonia. No wonder I was feeling very unwell. I had to endure lumber punctures and was kept in hospital for two weeks.

Over that time, I did get better gradually; however, I lost two stones in weight. Nicholas Eden, son of the 1950s Conservative Prime Minister Anthony Eden, was also patient at St Stephen's Hospital and close to death with AIDS. The ward staff laid on entertainment in the lounge for him and all of the other patients to enjoy. He had inherited the title of Earl of Avon after his father died in 1977. It was a posh affair with caviar and champagne. The main entertainment was a *Punch and Judy* show. Lord Avon died soon after I left the hospital. I was discharged and advised to complete my recovery at home and rest for four weeks.

I had just started to do some work on a customer's heating system before I was admitted to hospital. They needed a new boiler, and I had taken up the floorboards in their house to put new pipework in. Due to the meningitis, the job had been left unfinished so I decided to complete it as soon as I was allowed out of hospital. Cathy was willing to go with me to help out and get the job completed. She helped me to lift the boiler up on to the wall as I was still quite weak and poorly. With her help, I managed to finish the job. I was not aware that the customer had been back to his flat and saw that the work was not finished. He talked to his neighbour who informed him that I was in hospital. It was around this time that I decided I didn't want to use David's name any more. Since Mum and David changed it, I had always wanted to change it back again. It had been a while since I was away from their influence, and it felt easier to make the change now that I was living by my own rules. I reverted back to using my mother's maiden name, Jennings. I made the changes everywhere, except for on my school and college certificates. They had to remain as they were.

As my workload grew, I took on bigger projects. I only had my own intuition to guide me. Grandad and I talked about work, but he never offered me any advice on where I might have been going wrong, or how I could improve the way that I was running my business. I would have appreciated some guidance, but for some reason, he must have thought that it was better for me to figure it out myself. Throughout my life, I had looked up to him as a father figure and was always trying to prove to him that I was someone to be proud of, that I could do well in life. I had thought deep down that Grandad might have given me a position. I would have willingly worked for him in his heating company, but the offer never came. Despite this, I was doing very well in finding work off of my own back with lots of small jobs.

I started contracting for a small company whose owners chased the dream. They got a lot of large contracts, but as the jobs got bigger, the cash flow started to dry up and they began drip-feeding funds to keep the projects going. It started off with a big house in the Royal Borough of Kensington. The owner of the house was very particular about where things should be and fussed about everything. She constantly changed her mind at everyone's expense. There were a lot of extras and changes added to her bill, but when the work was completed, she didn't want to pay for it. I lost a lot of money on that job. Fortunately, I was still doing lots of small jobs that kept me afloat. The company took on an even bigger property in Hamilton Place, which took three months to complete. I thought that it was a good opportunity to make my money back. I was new at pricing bigger work and, in hindsight, I should have had a much bigger profit margin. Due to being relatively new to the trade, I relied on the experience of the two partners that were running the company. They kept all of my prices low and only gave me enough money to carry on. Cathy and I were hardly seeing each other due to our work commitments.

154

When we went out, it was with our own friends rather than together. Our relationship broke down, we drifted apart and I moved back in with Mum, David and my two sisters.

Turning the Tables

Living back with Mum and David was only a temporary arrangement until I could find somewhere else to live. Funds were really low as I was owed a considerable amount of money. I was working every hour that I could so that I could pay my supplies. It was Christmastime, and I made the decision to leave self-employment and seek work as an employee. I had become fed up with chasing people for money and wanted to go back to a less stressful life. I saved money to buy a house whilst back at my mum's. I wanted to move out again as soon as possible. I had become accustomed to my own space and moving back in with Mum and David felt like a step backwards. I didn't like David and preferred to spend as little time with him as possible. Even though we had had some kind of reconciliation in the past, we would never be friends. I needed my own space.

I picked up the Evening Standard newspaper and discovered that there were many relevant job listings that I could apply for. I did a bit of ringing around and a company called me back the next day. Someone was required to do commercial drainage work in St Thomas' Hospital. The supervisor was very interested when he found out that I had ran my own business and he appointed me as a supervisor. All of the stress that I had been feeling dissolved. I was back to getting paid on a weekly basis and was able to pay off the suppliers that I owed money to. I hadn't given up the ambition to return to working as a pipe fitter welder. But the fact that I had not done any welding since I was an apprentice was a bit of an issue, and I needed to take two welding exams.

Because I had been made up to supervisor, I was given a contract to manage for the Indonesian Embassy. It was quite a big contract, and I had been placed in charge of all of the plumbing. The company responsible for the heating and plant room was called Lorne Stewart. I got along really well with Peter Hoggett – he worked for the firm and managed the heating works. I wasn't very satisfied with the company that I was employed by and told Peter about my feelings. I was surprised and happy when he offered me the chance to come and work for Lorne Stewart as a pipe fitter. I accepted his offer and terminated my employment. I carried on working at the Indonesian Embassy with Peter, Grosvenor Square and many other contracts for the next four and a half years. My supervisor, Tony Saward, gave me opportunities whilst on-site to practise welding during my lunch breaks. I got to know a very good welder who was willing to give up his dinner breaks for me. It was amazing to watch him weld, and he had so much patience. He was very easy to get along with.

When I had to go to college to take my test, it was supposed to be for two days; one day to do the gas welding test and the other for the arc welding. I took all of my exams at my old college, Tottenham Technical. When I arrived in the workshop, I was informed that my company had cancelled one of my days. I could only take the welding test. I wanted both arc and gas so I phoned my office to see if they could book me back in for the second day. I was disappointed to hear that it was too late. I then had an idea and asked the examiners if I could take both tests on the same day. They told me that it had never been done before. I told them that I was confident I could do all six pieces and asked for a chance to do the arc test if I succeeded. The examiners agreed. The pressure was on, but I didn't let it get to me. I did the exam, and every piece was in the ninety percent grading bracket. I passed both exams in one day! The examiners seemed to be a bit shocked, but they were also happy that I had accomplished such a feat. I was very glad to be able to return to doing the work that I had loved the most. When I got back on-site, I couldn't thank my friend enough for all of his help. His name was Courtney Harriet. He was on-site first and also one of the first to go, but it wasn't to be our last encounter.

A New Start

There was a club in Croydon called Sinatra's Night Club. It was very popular because you only had to pay a fee to gain entry, which included all of the drinks too. My friends and I started to go there on a regular basis. The club had a strict, smart dress code. The doormen refused entry to anyone who was wearing trainers. Sometimes, they turned people away just because of the way that they were dressed or presented themselves. Sinatra's was a great place to meet new people and the dance floor was big. I met a woman called Terrie Holsgrove here one night whilst I was out with a group of friends. Terrie was also with a group of friends, and we got talking. We shared drinks at the bar and ended up on the dance floor, staying there for the rest of the night. When it was time to go, I asked Terrie if she would like a lift home and she accepted. We got along from the word go and started to date. We both enjoyed restaurants and spent a lot of time together enjoying meals out.

I had a friend that went out at the weekend clubbing with me. There were occasions where he stayed over after our nights out, and we returned home in the early hours of the morning. Mum used to let him sleep in the front room. Terrie started to spend more time at Mum's with me, too. It wasn't hard to notice David's displeasure. He hated the fact that I had returned and didn't like my friend sleeping over. I helped Mum out and bought shopping for her and my two sisters. Mum was quite happy for me to be around. She knew that David would not kick off in my presence.

One Saturday afternoon, my friend and I were sitting in the front room with David. Mum had just cooked David's dinner, and he must have forgotten for a moment that I was there. Something pricked his anger and he threw his loaded plate at the wall, creating a terrible mess. He slammed the tomato ketchup bottle hard onto the table that he was sitting at. David got up quickly and was about to storm out of the room in temper. But I intercepted him and pinned him against the wall before he could even get to the door. My friend was right

158

beside me too! I let David go, but he didn't do anything in retaliation. He just stormed out of the flat, walking hastily towards the lift in the outer corridor so we followed him. My friend was right in front of me, and he was directly behind David. My friend felt sorry for my mum. The way that David had just spoke to her was well out of order. He was angry about the way that David had behaved, too. Especially as my sister, Ann, was also in the flat at the time.

David's behaviour made something click inside of me. I recalled all of the nasty bullying that I had endured since I was a small child. It was as if all of the torment and spiteful actions that David had subjected me to over the years had all led to this moment in time. By the time, David had leant forward and extended his arm to push the lift button, my friend was right behindhim.

David must have sensed his closeness because he turned to look at him. Just as the lift had reached our floor and the door started to open, in the blink of an eye, my friend lunged forward with his closed fists and gave David an uppercut to the chin. His whole body lifted off of the ground and the force of the hit knocked him to the back of the open lift.

Claret started to run from David's nose, down his face and then off of his chin. It was dripping steadily onto his shirt. He appeared to be completely dazed with a look of shocked surprised on his face. His shaky legs gave way, causing him to slip and fall clumsily onto the lift floor. I was standing right beside my friend opposite the open door and, for a short moment, I wanted to go in there and finish what my friend had started. I could tell that my friend wanted to as well. But we both knew that if we did that, it would have been hard to stop. I looked to my friend and said, "Enough now." We both backed away from the lift and left David where he was. We went back to Mum's flat. My family and I were finally free from him, and I hoped that Mum would use the opportunity to live her life well from then on. I didn't see David again for quite a lot of years after that.

Because David was gone, I started spending more of my time with my mum. The atmosphere was completely different and Mum seemed much happier in herself. It was only a short while before Terrie and I moved in together at Mum's flat. Mum hadn't been in employment since we were living at Tyham close in Battersea, but she wanted to return to work so she started applying for jobs. For a short while, she had a managerial role doing dining cruises on the Thames and was earning a good wage too. I don't know the reason why Mum ended up leaving because she gave the impression that she really loved working there. Maybe it was because the hours that she worked were quite unsociable. They were a mixed bag of daytime and nightshifts any day of the week. Sometimes, there were big parties on the boats and Mum arrived home very late at night. After she had left the dining cruises, Mum made an application for a job with British Rail. She must have shown a good degree of competency as she was soon offered a supervisory role.

Terrie and I were ready to move out of Mum's place, and we started to view houses. Prices of homes in London were too expensive for our budget so we broadened our search area to Kent and came across a house in Chatham. It had just been fully renovated to a really good standard internally, but the garden had been neglected and needed a lot of work. Terrie and I liked the house and I liked to do gardening so we decided to buy it.

Before we moved out of Mum's flat, Terrie and I decided to go on holiday. It was Christmastime, and we booked a break to Benidorm in Spain. I thought that it would be nice to show Terrie the place that I used to go to when I was a small child. I was quite excited to go there again, too. When we arrived there, I did not recognise the place at all. Of course, I had expected some things to have changed, but everything looked completely different. I was a little disappointed that I could not involve Terrie in any reminiscence, but we still had a great holiday. One of the things that we both found funny was when Terrie went to buy some tomatoes from a fruit and veg stall. Her Spanish was not great, but she tried her best to communicate with the locals. Terrie had mistakenly asked the stallholder for two pounds of tomatoes. He put loads of them into two bags! Terrie and I looked towards one another without uttering a sound. Then she extended her hand out to the man and accepted the bags. She paid the man, said gracias and we walked away. When we returned to our apartment, we got out all of the bowls that we could find and filled them with the big, fresh tomatoes. They were dotted all over the place! We only cooked a few times during the holiday and took turns. We had tomatoes with every meal.

I told Terrie that I used to go to Spain in the sixties and then one more time in 1971. I remember that our family used to leave our apartment in the evenings and go to a local hotel to enjoy their entertainments. I remember a New Year's Eve when the hotel put on a big party for its guests. Non-guests were expected to pay a £10 entry fee, but because we were regular users of the hotel's bar and restaurant, we were welcomed and treated as guests. I remember it to have been a really good night, especially as I knew that it came at no cost at all. I've always thought of the free things in life as being the best.

Making a Family

We were back and ready to move into our new home. It was a two-bedroom house. Terrie had become pregnant sometime around the beginning of August 1989, and in May 1990, we had a baby boy whom we named Grant. In May the following year, we had another son, and we called him Adam. They both had my surname, Jennings. It was the start of the recession and Lorne Stewart had already laid off a lot of welders. I was the nineteenth left on the company. At the time, bank interest rates were the highest that they had ever been at fifteen percent. Almost every penny of our earnings was going towards the mortgage. We weren't the only family that was struggling at the time. Many lost their homes. It was a very stressful time for Terrie and I so we decided to move back to London so that we could be nearer to our families. After three and a half years, Terrie and I surrendered the house back to the mortgage company and deposited the keys back through the letterbox when we left. We were both very sad to have to do that, but we had no other choice.

Back in London, we secured temporary accommodation in the London Borough of Southwark, then not long after that we were offered a permanent flat. It wasn't long after we settled in that I was laid off of work. I was devastated because I had liked working for Lorne Stewart very much and they were one of the better companies around at the time. I had also learned a great deal during my time in employment. The unions were very strong. It was only a short while before I received a letter from them.

I began work for a company in the London Borough of Southwark. How Engineering was based in Bermondsey Street, and they had just gained a massive contract in Southampton, Sussex. It came at a good time for them because there were a lot of people seeking new employment in the trade. In return for the union's assistance, everyone who went on to work for that contractor was made to join. It was one of the biggest sites that I had ever worked on. Because it was so far away from home, I found lodgings there. I didn't have a lot of choice really. I had to do it to stay in employment. There were around two hundred pipe fitters and welders on the job, the most that I had ever seen. Five of us rented a house together, just outside of Southampton. Many of us had never experienced so much time away from our families and we were desperate to get back to London to work. We found it very hard at times.

The only ones that owned mobile phones were those who had a lot of money. None of us had one, but there were two land phones on-site, next to the cabin. The queues were so long at breakfast time! Workers were using them to call jobs in London so there was practically no chance of using them then. I encountered another welder working down there, my old friend Courtney, who had helped me a few years previously by giving up his time in order to help me back into welding. We were very pleased to see each other again. We worked together in one of the workshops that were set up around the site.

We were to stay there for the next seven months before being able to work back in London and being back with Terrie and our boys, Grant and Adam. Mum had recently moved from Southfields with her new chap that she was seeing. She owned the flat in Southfields, and it had earned her enough money to purchase a house in Leatherhead, Surrey. Up to this point, I had been getting on quite well with her, but I didn't like the chap that she was with. You could say that Mum had leapt out of the frying pan and into the fire. One day, she asked me if I would do some work on her garden shed. It needed a new roof, but she didn't want to pay too much money on it and asked me to fix it in the cheapest way possible. It looked okay at first, but the rain made the sheeting bubble up. Mum's partner and I had a fall out over it. That was the last time that I saw her. Shortly after the shed dispute, she moved again, but I was never told where to. My sisters later told me that Mum had moved to Spain. To this day, I have never seen or heard from her.

How Engineering had a couple of jobs back in London. I was asked if I wanted to go to the one at Smithfield's in the city. I couldn't say yes quick enough. Being back in London meant that I could go home to my family every night. Work was picking up slowly. I started to work for different agencies as the pay was much better. Bringing home a good wage meant that I could take Terrie and the boys on holiday a few times a year. If I didn't have any work, I put cards in shop windows offering removals services. I did deliveries for Terrie's dad too. I even did a bit of floor and wall tiling to get by. I continued to work for agencies for the next three years fitting boilers, pumps, pipework and plant.

I wanted a change from building sites to maintenance, maintaining plant and gas burner engineering. The company that I was working for at the time won a contract from the council. They gave me the opportunity to repair and maintain domestic boilers in people's homes. I started to study books about boilers and gas appliances. I was glad to be working with Courtney again. I had missed my friend and was glad when I discovered that he had decided to go in the same direction as me. We were working on gas appliances and took the exams together. We both passed.

I had been seeing Aunt Ciss regularly, but our time together dwindled when she retired. Due to no longer being in employment, Aunt Ciss had found a new way of getting out and socialising. She was finding great enjoyment in attending tea dances and went out most weekends. Nine times out of ten, Terrie and I turned up to discover that Aunt Ciss was not at home. There was one particular Saturday when Terrie and I caught her just as she was coming out of her front door and opened the wooden garden gate. We had just turned into the street and noticed her wearing her coat and brown leather gloves which matched her shoes. Her red and black silk scarf was covering her curled hair. She always wore those outerclothes when she was going out.

Terrie wound her window down as she was closest to my aunt. We could tell that she was in a rush to go somewhere. Aunt Ciss leant down with her face towards the window and said, "Can't stop, I'm on my way to a tea dance and I'm running a bit late!" Neither of us had time to respond because she started to run away from in the opposite direction. We were watching her teeter along the pavement, and she only got about twenty yards before she tripped on an uneven paving slab, stumbling forwards. There was a moment of concern, and we could see that she had scraped one of her knees. But Aunt Ciss got up from the ground very quickly, waved and shouted back in a laughing voice, "I'm all right!" Then she carried on with her journey! Terrie and I looked towards each other in amazement and shook our heads. After that, I always called ahead to make sure that my aunt was at home. I often visited her after work as I knew that I would probably catch her indoors then. We talked to each other on the phone often, and over time, this became our main way of staying in contact. I got letters from her too. I enjoyed receiving them.

I began to notice that Aunt Ciss was becoming increasingly forgetful. It was mostly little things at first. I learned that she had dementia. Her neighbour told me that she had noticed the changes in Aunt Ciss' behaviour too. I had never heard about dementia before as I had not known anyone living with it in the past. I had no experience and didn't know how to deal with it. Over the years that followed, the conversations changed somewhat. It saddened me that I could no longer ask my aunt for the advice which had been so invaluable to me throughout my life. I think that this must have been a sad and frustrating situation for her too. Aunt Ciss had always been so independent, especially since Uncle Ernie had died. She realised that she could no longer live alone and decided to move to sheltered accommodation. My three of my boys came to assist with the move. Lawrence was working for a removals company in Fulham at the time. He helped by supplying boxes and packing materials and gave us all a lesson in how to pack properly.

The transition wasn't too bad for my aunt because she already had several friends living there who were enjoying the lifestyle. The management arranged coach trips to the seaside and residents holidayed together. One of the places that they stayed at Folkestone in Kent. The residents lived in one bedroom bungalows which were close to Red Post Hill in Dulwich. However, there was a large communal lounge where the residents were able to socialise together. I took Terrie and the kids to visit Aunt Ciss at her bungalow and also invited her on days out with the family. One time, we went to a theme park, Chessington World of Adventures. On Sundays, I often took Aunt Ciss for a roast lunch with my family at a very nice local pub called The Fox on the Hill. They were good times. Looking back, I feel that Aunt Ciss might have been better off staying at her old home. It probably would have been better for her memory, but I only understood this after she had moved.

I had turned thirty-six when I decided that it was to be my last year playing rugby union and rugby netball. I received an injury to the top part of my arm in the previous year. It was quite a serious injury because I ripped a muscle, and it had left me in constant pain. It had become difficult to throw the ball or go in hard on a tackle. The final match that I played was in the summer. It was the last one of the rugby netball season and the referee had placed the ball in between myself and a player on the opposing side. One of us had to win the ball, and I had already beaten him a few times during the match. He didn't like it. Instead of going for the ball, the other player decided to go for my ankles and he grabbed them hard. He swiftly lifted my entire body into the air and threw me backwards over his shoulders! I didn't expect him to do it and had no time to react. He was shorter than me so it was easy for him to get underneath me. I landed hard and quite awkwardly onto my head and neck as I hit the ground with a huge thump. As I laid on my back, I could not move my body, only my eyes. That moment seemed to last forever, and it was quite worrying to me. I could see the other players' faces above me. They were all asking if I was okay. But about ten minutes later, I had managed to get back up onto my feet, and I carried on with the game. I wasn't giving up that easily. Because it was the last game of the season, we went the Windmill pub on the common afterwards.

My younger two boys had watched me play that evening, and they came to the pub with me. I was feeling fine, and we had a good time. But we didn't stay for too long, and after a couple of pints, we made our way home. When I had a shower later that evening, I came over all funny. I was finding it extremely difficult to stand upright properly and had to hold onto the walls all the way to my bedroom to stop myself from falling over again. I went to bed to sleep it off, but I should have stayed awake because I was concussed. I seemed well again when I got up the next morning. I feel quite lucky that it wasn't more serious. However, the experience and the fact that I was feeling a lot of pain throughout my body encouraged me to make the decision to stop playing field sports.

Bowling

It didn't take me much time to find a safer and less strenuous sport to take up. Surrey Keys Bowling Alley had recently been newly built. Terrie and I decided to take the boys along to have a bit of family fun, and we all enjoyed it immensely. We met a woman there who was a regular bowler. She had bowled in different leagues in the past and she wanted to set up her own league at Surrey Keys. When she asked me if I would like to take part, I happily accepted her offer. Terrie's brother was keen to be my bowling partner in doubles. When the season finished, we came second place. I thought that it was a great achievement. I enjoyed bowling so much that I wanted to learn more about the game and improve on my own techniques.

A member from one of the other teams that bowled in our league told me about Lewisham AMF. He took part in the leagues there and suggested that it would be a good place to bowl and learn about the game. I decided to join a league there and was glad of my decision because the lanes were dressed for league bowling and an excellent environment to learn. I received a great deal of support from fellow bowlers and improved my game rapidly. The more I learned, the better I became. I was invited to join a five-man team to enter a competition at Lewisham AMF. I was bowling well for a beginner and had a high handicap. The rest of the team were all scratch bowlers – they had no handicap. The winners were to go on to compete in the finals at Nottingham AMF, and we were all hopeful for victory. We played really well and won the tournament on the day, which allowed us to gain our place in the finals. I was very happy with my own performance and went home well chuffed with myself.

I found out that the prize was the best that had ever been known. The winners would get the opportunity to play in Las Vegas. The cost of the flights and apartment or hotel were part of the prize as well as the opportunity to win money and even more prizes. Myself and the rest of the team went to

Nottingham for a long weekend. We played all day and late into the evening. We played hard and the days seemed to go on forever. Once play had finished, I came sixth place in the tournament with my handicap. As a team, we just missed out, but we were still in the top ten. The buzz made me want to play more and enter more tournaments. I was completely hooked.

I started to go for regular bowling coaching on Saturday mornings. I was fully committed and wanted to learn everything about the sport. I even got my family playing, and the two boys bowled in youth teams on Saturday mornings. Grant had a natural talent, and his game improved immensely. He went on to win the doubles with another boy. Grant and I became very good friends with him. When I was at the peak of my game, I had become a high-average (scratch) bowler. During those years, I had always attained first, second or third position in all of the leagues that I competed in. I was also team captain in the majority of those leagues. There were times when I missed out on the top score with one spare. I averaged over 250 points out of a top score of 300.

Understanding

It was 2012 when I received a call from an unknown number. I answered it and was surprised to hear that it was Mum's cousin, Pat. I was actually quite shocked to hear from her at all and knew instantly that she had contacted me to give me bad news about my Aunt Ciss (Carol). Pat informed me that Aunt Ciss had passed away and that her funeral was to be held at Norwood Cemetery in South West London. Aunt Ciss had lived to the ripe old age of ninety-two. Even so, the news was still sad and unexpected. I felt emotionally upset and had to sit down because my legs started to shake uncontrollably. Aunt Ciss was the first person that I went to whenever I needed an answer for something that was playing on my mind. I always got the response that I needed. Aunt Ciss had been more of a mother to me than Mum ever was.

Around that time, I felt ready to enter bowling competitions against other counties. I wanted to bowl for London. To do so, I had to play at Lewisham AMF, where the London counties were held. It was roughly two or three weeks before the qualifying games were due to be held that I had learned the tragic news of my aunt's death. My bowling ability went to pot, and I was not able to score any higher than 150. My mind was no longer on bowling. I bowled in the league for that season and haven't bowled since.

I attended my aunt's funeral with my partner and my boys. It was important to me to show my respects and say my goodbyes to a woman that I had loved all of my life. I always will. My aunt's death changed my life but had no idea that her death would reveal the truth about who my father is or was. Members of my extended family were already standing outside the chapel when we arrived at the cemetery. Everyone was wearing black out of respect and talking amongst themselves. Nobody really noticed us as we got out of the car. A lot of people didn't know who I was. We made our way over to join the rest of the family, and I recognised Mum's cousin Pat first. Pat was talking to another woman who had her back to us so she did not see us as we walked in her direction. I announced myself and my family to Pat and then the woman who was looking away from us turned around and introduced herself. She was Mum's cousin, Margaret. I had not seen her since I was a young boy. Aunt Ciss used to tell me that Margaret was the black sheep of the family. I noticed that Margaret was looking at me in the same way that Hilda used to look at me as I arrived to visit at the bungalow.

Margaret was staring intently, as if she was checking out every single detail. She couldn't stop staring at me with the look of disbelief. I think it was because she could see my father in me. We got talking and I said, "So you're the black sheep of the family."

Margaret replied in a serious tone, "No, Mark, you're the black sheep of the family." I could tell that she really did mean it, too. I was speechless at the time and just laughed it off. I didn't understand what she had meant by calling me the black sheep! However, I was soon to find out, and I could never have imagined how much of a shock it would be to me, my partner and our boys.

Margaret and I talked some more, and I could sense that she had something important to tell me. I was not surprised when she then went on to invite me to her house for Sunday lunch. I accepted. This was one of the most emotional days that I had ever experienced. I saw my aunt laid to rest at the church and said my final goodbyes. Sitting there, in front of her coffin, I remembered all of the good times; the hot holidays that we shared, our times together throughout our lives, her husband Ernie. I remembered how she had given me Uncle Ernie's gloves and scarves, which had made me feel quite special and privileged at the time because she had never given his personal belongings to anyone else. I really thought a lot of her and appreciated her nurturing ways towards me.

I went to Margaret's house on a Sunday afternoon with my son, Grant. We spoke a lot about family Aunt Ciss had kept me up to date with what had been going on in people's lives over the years. Margaret was unaware of this so some of the things that she told me was old news, but she also told me some really interesting information like the older history of Mum's family and our family tree. For the first time, I was told that my great-grandparents had been called Thomas and Marjorie Frohock. I knew in my heart that Margaret had the answer that I was desperately seeking. I looked at her and asked her directly "Who is my father?" She paused for a short while and then looked at her daughter, who shook her head as if to say 'no'. I didn't notice Margaret's daughter do that, but Grant did as he was sitting right beside her. Margaret then uttered the name Edward Martin and nothing else was said after that. I had no reason to doubt her in that moment so I believed her.

In the sixties, Margaret's cousin, Edward, had lived above the Bobby Moore shop at Upton Park. He was married to Tina Moore's cousin, Jennifer Cox, in 1967. Edward was no longer alive at this time though. He had passed away a few years before. The last time that I saw Edward was at St Thomas' Hospital when I was visiting my Aunt Ciss. He shook my hand to greet me. You can tell a lot from a handshake. I knew that he was not my father as soon as Margaret said his name. But she then started to talk about Bobby Moore and how he and Edward were very close friends. Margaret said that I should take a look at Edward's photos that he had had taken with Bobby. There was one photo in particular that was mentioned of them both together. She told me to have a look online too, so I did that as soon as I got home.

Unfortunately, I didn't find the photo that Margaret had described. However, I did find other photos where it was hard not to notice the similarities that Bobby and I shared. Our bone structure, shape of our mouths, noses and our blue eyes. Margaret had cleverly pointed me in the direction of the truth without explicitly telling me the answers herself. Up until this point, I had no idea that Bobby Moore might be my father. I had always thought that he was just a friend of the family. I then realised that I had resembled Bobby so much as a child that they must have just looked at me and couldn't help talking about our similarities. All of my family members had called me 'special' throughout my life. But believe me when I say that I had never felt special. Not one bit! Margaret kindly encouraged me to go and see Grandad, and I decided to do it.

It had been a decade since I last spent time Grandad and Hilda. I informed Margaret that I had not seen him for many years. I wanted to find out how he and Hilda were and wanted him to tell me who my father was.

The last time had been on a sunny, Sunday afternoon in 2002. I took my two boys along with me to visit their great-grandparents. Grant was eleven and Adam was ten. I hadn't visited them as often as I would have liked to. Life was hectic with work six, sometimes seven days a week. On Saturday afternoons, I was still playing rugby at Merton. During this particular visit, Grandad gave each of the boys a golf club and a bucket of golf balls. He took them to the garden, showed them how to tee off and then we left them to it. I went to sit in the conservatory with Grandad, and we had a catch-up conversation, picking up from our last encounter. After a bit of time had passed, Grandad returned to the garden to see that the boys had torn up the grass with the golf clubs that he had given them. He wasn't too impressed! He snatched the golf clubs from both of the boy's hands and then shoved them back at them again! He spoke in a harsh voice, "Now take them home with you."

I replied, saying, "Yes! I'm taking them home, and we're not coming back!"

Whilst journeying to see Grandad I thought about our previous encounter. I wasn't sure of the reception that I would receive, and it had taken me a bit of courage to go there. It snowed very hard in Surrey, and a thick layer had settled on the ground. Everything was white, and it looked like a scene off of an old-fashioned Christmas card. I approached the driveway slowly, looking towards the bungalow. It still looked the same as I remembered it, and I thought about all of the previous times that Hilda had come outside to greet me. The driveway could be seen from the front window so she could tell when someone had arrived. But she did not come out. I was hoping that everything would be the same as it had been before, and I was a bit surprised that I didn't see her. I stepped out of my car and walked towards the door with all kinds of thoughts in my head, wondering what kind of greeting that I would receive. I felt nervous about coming home. I knocked on his door, and after a little while, Grandad opened it with a surprised greeting. "Hello, you!" That's how he always greeted me, never by my first name. It was as if I'd only been away for a short while. Grandad invited me in.

Grandad was ninety years old. He had aged somewhat since our last encounter, and I noticed his frailty. He had had quite a large stature as a younger man. But I could see that he had shrunk quite a few inches, probably due to his hip replacements and his old age. He needed home assistance and had carers to do some things, like bringing in hot meals. We went together into the kitchen, where his carer had just put his meal onto the table. Just before we both sat down, I told him that I had seen Margaret and that she had told me my father was Edward Martin. I then sat on a chair at the end. Grandad sat down at the other end so hard that I thought that his chair would break. He leant across the small, yellow-topped dining table towards me and said, "Bloody family, can't stand them!" The way that Grandad said this gave me the impression that he knew that Margaret had said a lie. I knew it was a lie, even though the tale

172

about Edward Martin being my father went around the family when I was a kid. But I didn't say that to Grandad because I wanted to hear it from him!

I asked Grandad where Hilda was and he told me that she had sadly passed away a year and a half ago. Hilda had always been very good to me and had given me a lot of her time and attention. From then on, I visited Grandad as often as I could. He became very unwell and spent bouts of time in hospital. During his last five months, I brought family members to see him. Like Grandad had been, I was a heating engineer so it was easy to talk about work related stuff like plant and boilers that I had worked on.

I had earned good money back in the sixties and that prosperity continued and increased throughout his working life. He went from being self-employed one-man band to owning quite a reasonable company. It had two other partners who brought money into the business whilst Grandad took care of the staff and contracts. Central heating was becoming more common in the 1970s so for Grandad this was a boom period. We chatted a lot, but I found it extremely difficult to raise discussions about things to do with the family. He didn't want to talk about it. I said to Grandad, "I need to know." Grandad knew what I meant, and I was disappointed that he responded by saying that his mum always told him never to tell. I replied that his mum was no longer around anymore, but I was.

Grandad and I liked to go out together for dinner to his favourite pub, the one that he visited with Hilda when she was alive. He had struggled to walk since he had had two hip replacements and was finding it increasingly difficult. During one of the pub visits, I walked to the men's room with Grandad.

He turned towards me and asked, "What do you want from me?"

I replied back to him, "Your love."

He then looked at me with a happy expression and said, "I can give you that," and continued walking towards the men's room. When we were later alone in his house, Grandad asked me for my forgiveness. I gave it without hesitation, even though I was not sure what part of my life he was referring to. Maybe he was asking for forgiveness because he had promised Nan Rose that he would give me an apprenticeship in his company, and that I would inherit it when he passed. He promised Nan Rose that I would be in his will and that I would be looked after. But none of this happened. Grandad had cut me out of his estate years ago, and it seemed that now he wanted to make amends. But I had never gone to see Grandad about money. I only wanted him to tell me that

Bobby was my father. Grandad asked me to move back in with him, but I declined as I had my own home by then. I wasn't aware at the time, but it was to be the last time that I saw him.

Grandad was receiving around-the-clock care and was ninety-one years old at the time of my final visit. I had been sitting with him, holding his frail hand, laughing and joking. I've got a very dry sense of humour, and our chit-chat was making him laugh. We had not done this together for many years, and it was one of the things that I had missed. On this particular day, he was quite chirpy. Grandad was standing in the front room doorway when he said to me, "Who do you remind me of?"

I replied, "Your brother, Arthur?"

To which, Grandad replied, "No." Out of all of the brothers, Grandad and Arthur had been the closest. Arthur was a right character!

Then I said, "My dad, Bobby Moore." Grandad didn't need to say anything because his body language did the talking.

He dropped his head and shoulders, then mumbled, "I remember your dad as a footballer."

I replied back, "You remember him more than just a football player." I believed that Grandad had had dealings with Bobby over the years. Grandad didn't say anything else. He didn't need to. I had finally got the answer that I wanted. It had taken him five months to disclose who my father was. I asked him why he let me go when I lived with him as a child. Why did he have to give me back when I didn't want to go back? Grandad said that it was because of outside influences and that he had to give me back. It made me assume that someone had made him return me. I am quite sure that it was not my mother.

The day after my visit, Grandad was admitted back into hospital. I was unable to go and see him for two weeks. It was the busiest time for me at work, servicing and repairing broken down boilers. When I arrived at the hospital, he couldn't be found, and when the records were checked, I discovered that he had passed away the day before. I couldn't believe that Graham Jennings didn't have the courtesy to tell me! Anyone ought to be able to imagine how upset I was at finding out about my grandfather's death in this way. I cried all the way home. Grandad had been an important figure for much of my life. Especially before I found out who my biological father was, as he had filled the gap that not having a father around had created.

Myself and other family members attended Grandad's funeral. It was the second major funeral in two years. Most of those who turned up were the people who had been written into the will. Graham should have made changes, but he wanted to be the main beneficiary. But when his wife had divorced him and took all that she needed, Graham needed Grandad's money to keep him in the lifestyle that he was accustomed to.

It was during this time that I learned some more about the painting in the bungalow depicting the man in the chair with the young girl. Graham pointed to the painting, which was actually a print, and told me that the duo depicted in it was Grandad and Mum. I think that Hilda and Graham had both been trying to tell me that Mum was his little girl, whom he spoiled and loved dearly and gave anything that she desired. I know that Mum had a lot of jewellery. There's no doubt in my mind that Mum was 'Daddy's little girl' and that they had been very close. Mum had dressed smartly until she met David. She would always tell me that I was special, and that I would have no worries when I got older. Mum said that I had been conceived in Italy in 1963.

When I had a conversation with my mum's cousin, Robert Jennings, he told me that I should speak to Tina Moore's cousin, Jennifer. He told me that I was a Moore, too. I decided to seek the help of someone who was an expert in researching family trees. I wanted to find out what the family connections were between the Moore family and Edward Martin and Jennifer Cox's family (the Frohocks). From the age of seven, I had been kept away from the Moore family and the Martin family, but I never understood why until recently.

I had inherited some old photographs from my late Aunt Ciss. Looking at them all together, it was clear to see how close my relationship with Nan Rose and Aunt Ciss had been. As I went through them individually, I started to mentally put names to the faces. One particular photograph stood out more than the others. It was a family photograph that had been taken outside a restaurant in Spain. My mother was seated on the far left, two feet to the right was Martin Peters and sat beside him was Tina Moore. I was sitting in front of Tina and my Aunt Ciss. We spent so much time together and that shows how close we were as a family.

I needed to prove to myself that I am the true son of Bobby Moore. Without a question, we have facial similarities, but looking like someone doesn't mean that you are related. I looked online at family photographs of the Moores. I noticed that they were the same people that were captured in some of my own photographs. Picking them up and examining them, I started to slowly put more names to the faces. It took me a little time to realise that they were the same people that I had known as a small boy. There was one photograph of a young girl and I with Bobby sitting behind us both. All three of us were grinning and looked really happy together. I remembered that the girl used to be my best friend when we were small and that we were together a lot back then. Her name was Roberta Moore, my half-sister! I never knew that at the time.

To me, Bobby had only ever been a friend of the family. I knew that he was Roberta and Dean's dad, but I never, ever guessed that he might have been my dad too. Even if he hadn't had been my biological father, we were still a family member through marriage. When Tina Dean and Bobby Moore got married in 1962, my mum's cousin, I believe that it was Edward who gave Tina away. Tina gave him the nickname 'Dreaded Eddie'. Even though the truth had been covered over with lies, they were now backing up the truth. Mum said that the Grange Manor Farm belonged to the company that she worked for and that it was a place for employees to go on holiday to. But I discovered that it didn't belong to the company that Mum worked for at all. It was owned by West Ham United Football Club at the time. In the sixties, we went to Spain every year. Mum used to tell me that we holidayed in Benidorm, Costa Blanca. But we didn't stay anywhere Benidorm.

The resort was called Platja de L'Estartit, which was in Costa Brava. No wonder, I didn't recognise anywhere or anything in Benidorm! I was such a young boy when we used to go to Spain that the family must have thought that I wouldn't remember. But I did. That's why I was confused when I went to Benidorm with Terrie. I was even living with Mum at that time and commented to her that I was looking forward to revisiting the area. But Mum never said a thing about it, even when I came home and told her about my disappointment. I had been fed a red herring! It all made sense at last.

One afternoon, I sat down to watch a documentary about the Terracotta Army in China. Every one of them is unique and each soldier's individual characteristics have been immortalised in the pottery. The narrator mentioned ears and explained that just like in real life, each of the terracotta soldier's ears were unique. This information sparked interest in my mind and prompted me to do my own research. I learned that when it comes to the genetics of our ear shape, we only have one gene from our mother and one gene from our father. The father's genes are typically stronger and are passed down to their offspring. I did even more research into the DNA of the ear. Sometimes people construct family trees out of photographs that they have taken of the person when they were young and then again around ten years later. This shows how the ears have grown over time. Then the parent's photographs can be added to compare the shape, curves of the lobes and bone structure. It's shocking what can be discovered.

When I was forming my own ear family tree, I used the internet to search for photographs of Bobby's family photos and came across and old black and white photograph that had Bobby and his father in it. They were both looking to the left and Bobby was a young boy at the time. Both of their ears on the left side matched. I put an image of my left ear to theirs, and it was a perfect match. During the Great War, families were separated and then reunited after many months, or even years. These physical traits were used to find and identify loved ones. It was well before blood DNA could be used. I believe that some modern court cases where blood DNA has not been available were won in this way. This is the definitive proof that I needed for myself. When it dawned on me that the people in the photographs and the Moore people were in fact the same people, I had to sit back and let it sink in. It was the moment when I discovered that the family I had been searching for had been my family all along.

My mother, Maureen, and Edward were cousins, which was exactly the same situation as Jennifer's relationship. That meant that the Frohocks became part of the larger Moore family. Edward A Martin married Jennifer C Cox in 1967 in the London Borough of Redbridge. They moved into the flat above the Bobby Moore's Sports Shop. Jennifer Cox was born in 1945 in Ilford. Her mother's maiden name was Wild.

Sometime in the same year, a new tenant (or indeed a lodger!) by the name of Mr John J Squibb arrived, and soon after that, things began to go wrong in Edward and Jennifer's marriage. It seems that Jennifer and Mr Squibb started a secret relationship. They may have already been in a relationship when he moved in. Edward and Jennifer decided to end their marriage and got divorced. In 1972, Edward married Janet Watmore in Falmouth, Cornwall. Jennifer had also moved on, and she married the former lodger, Mr J (W) Squibb in Havering, Essex. The marriage was registered in the second quarter of 1973.

Mental Breakdown

Since losing Aunt Ciss my mental health had taken a dive and I started to break down. Work had been very unsupportive. I rang my manager to inform him that my aunt had passed away and I needed to take time off so that I could attend her funeral. He only allowed me one day, rather than the two weeks that I should have been allowed. He knew how close I was to her! No sooner had the phone call ended, I felt the dark cloud of depression coming over me. I didn't stop crying for more than two hours.

When I lost Grandad a year later, I suffered even more. The two people who had loved and protected me the most throughout my life were no longer around, and I missed them deeply. I was living alone in Kent at that time in my life. Terrie and I were still in a very strong relationship even though we were not living together. I had made the decision to live apart because we got along much better that way. Terrie would have liked it if I was living with her, but I preferred the silence around me and the newfound space within my head.

My childhood had started to catch up with me. In all of the time that we had been together, I had never discussed much of it with her. In fact, I had never explained anything to anyone. I did tell Terrie about the holidays that I had enjoyed with my family in Spain as a small child. Terrie asked in surprise, "What, in the sixties?"

To which I replied, "Yes, didn't you?" It had never crossed my mind that it was something out of the ordinary.

Terrie then said, "Mark, there weren't that many people who could afford to go on holiday to Spain, especially on a plane. And you went quite a lot." I had never considered how privileged I actually was back then. The holidays in Spain and the fact that David is not my biological father are the only things that I told Terrie about. I definitely did not want to share any memories of my time living with David. I didn't ever speak to her about Bobby being in my life as a young boy because I didn't realise its significance.

My aunt's death had coincided with a certain amount of buying going on the company that I was working for. The company was taken to court by several different people who were employed by them and the company was losing the cases. I also received a certain amount of bullying in the two years since my aunt's death, and it pushed me over the edge. I suffered a mental breakdown. I was tearful often and couldn't stop myself from crying. My manager noticed my emotional state and encouraged me to do something about it. He referred me to talk to one of the company's doctors by phone.

I was sitting in my car on one of the company's sites that we maintain when I received the call. It didn't feel as if my conversation with the doctor had made me feel any better. In fact, I felt much worse and had serious thoughts about ending my life right there and then. I got out of my car and made my way up to the top of the building that we were maintaining. I walked to the end of the rooftop and stood there, with the ends of my feet protruding over the edge. I knew full well that if I made the decision to jump that it would be final, and I spent over an hour playing the game 'Should I, shouldn't I' in my mind. I thought hard about the family that I still had around me and how unfair it would have been for them to lose me. I couldn't bring myself to deny my sons the opportunity to have a father around. I knew myself what not having a father around was like and didn't want them to be without me. I thought about Terrie and my grandchildren. I didn't want to hurt them either.

My boss was present when I had an emotional breakdown in front of my co-workers. It had only happened a few days before I contemplated jumping off of the rooftop. He should have given me time off of work, but he never even offered it to me. Nobody understood the mental stresses that I had endured since Aunt Ciss' death because I hadn't discussed them with anyone. The only family member that I ever disclosed my suicide attempt to was my son, Grant. Life carried on as usual.

I left that company and made a fresh start. Terrie helped me immensely to get back to my old self. I was able to get back on track with her unwavering support, which to this day, I am still thankful for to the bottom of my heart. In the years that followed my breakdown, I still had a few moments when I was alone, indoors. It wasn't uncommon in those instances for me to drink a whole bottle of rum. I even took drugs in a bid to block out the memories, but it just made me worse.

Stories from Other People

Those who knew both my mum and Bobby have all told me the same thing. Mum was in Bobby's company often. Also that she and Bobby were very fond of each other and that they both enjoyed their time together. Whilst I was with another engineer doing some routine maintenance work in London, we got talking to the porter of the building that we were both working in. His name was Liam. The apartment block was in Kensington area. Liam was in his seventies and had worked as a porter since a young age. He started portering in a block of apartments on the corner of Baker Street and Euston Road. The apartments are still there today and can be distinguished by their green coloured windows. I realised instantly that those apartments were the same ones that I had visited with Mum and Bobby as a small child.

Liam went on to say that even though there was a lift Bobby chose not to use it when Mum was with him. Bobby had an apartment on the fourth floor and they walked up the stairs instead. Liam said that he watched them walk to the stairs. Bobby walked in front, then turned his head to snigger at Mum as she walked towards him, then she carried on up the stairs beside him. I believed that he was telling me the truth because he stopped me and said that he knew my mum and dad as soon as I mentioned Bobby. I was actually shocked at that revelation. I asked him, "If you know who my mum is, describe her to me." His response shocked me. He described her spot-on.

Someone unknown to me uploaded a photograph of Mum with Bobby in Bobby's archives. She is sat upon Bobby's lap whilst giving him a loving kiss on his cheek. Bobby's eyes are closed and the expression on his face says it all. In another photograph, Tina and Bobby are in a similar pose, but Bobby doesn't have the same loving expression that he had with Mum. The way that Mum and Grandad Charlie used to go on about Italy made it sound as if Mum wanted to run away with Bobby forever. That was in 1963, one year after Bobby married Tina. In 1971, Mum's life changed forever. She would no longer see the man that she obviously loved so dearly, and it made her a broken woman. Bobby was put onto a pedestal after winning the World Cup in 1966, and England have never brought the Cup home since. Nobody was ever to find out about the love that Mum and Bobby had for each other.

There was something else that I discovered when I looked through my photographs. One of them captured a moment where members of my family were seated with a man by the name of Peter Bonetti. Peter played as goal keeper for Chelsea Football Club in the seventies. The group was sitting together around a small table and Peter was wearing a large Spanish hat called a sombrero. There was an old wine or champagne bottle in the centre of the table with a lit candle. The wax had run down the neck and onto the sides of the bottle. It looked as if the bottle had been used many times for this purpose. The table looked rustic, as if it had been fashioned from an old, wooden wine or beer barrel that had been cut down to make a table top. It had three legs fitted to the bottom. Nan Rose could be seen sitting to the right of Peter. Nan was also wearing a sombrero. Aunt Ciss was seated to the left of Peter, whilst Uncle Ernie was sitting next to her on the other side. I noticed myself in the image too, laying asleep behind Nan. It has Spanish handwriting on the reverse side and is dated 26 September 1969. Peter's birthday was on the 27. I like to think that we were part of the celebration.

It was then that I realised why I used to go and watch Chelsea play. I always felt as if I had somehow known Peter Bonetti. This photographs proved that I had known him. Someone had written something in a foreign language on the back. I wondered if it might have been Bobby so I googled his signature so that I could make a comparison. I noticed straightaway that the style was very much the same. I also noticed that part of the signature did not look right. It didn't look like it said Moore at all. It looked like my own name, Mark. I then went on to search for an example that was from before I was born. It was in fact different and could clearly be seen as Moore. After 1964, Bobby dropped one O and crossed the E. The extra line on the E made it look like a K. It looks as if Bobby used this signature for the rest of his life. I believe that Bobby was the person who gave me my name, not my mum. It is my opinion that he must have loved me very much, and I like to think that he was using his signature as a way to tell me that I am his son. That means so much to me.

Bobby and I have a lot in common. He would run three times a week, play squash, and chess. So did I! From the age of thirteen to thirty-six, I played rugby, from school level to club level. I could have played football, but I much more preferred the physical aspect of rugby. Until I started to write this book, I did not realise exactly how much I have enjoyed sports. I have taken part in many sporting activities, some of which haven't even got a mention. I have always sought to be a high achiever and revelled in being 'part of the team'. This all came naturally to me – it's in my blood.

I've repaired many boilers and heating systems inside people's homes in and around Essex over the years. I'm a sociable person and enjoyed having a chin-wag with the customers. The subject of football often came up and we sometimes discussed things like what team we supported. I always replied that I didn't support any football teams. There were some times when I could not help myself and I told them who my father was. Of course, the customers were intrigued about my story and how I made my discoveries. They sometimes remarked the facial similarities between Bobby and I, mainly similarities in our face and head shape. Some commented on how they thought that we have the same bone structure. Those who knew Bobby in person told me their memories of the times that they had spent in Bobby's company. I was glad to be told nothing but good things, and it made me happy to hear about them. Those conversations gave me a better understanding of the man that I now call my father. I often think about the life that I had as a young boy and how it still affects me every day. It has been hard for me to keep the thoughts that are on my mind to myself, especially at the beginning of my discovery journey.

One of the most memorable stories that I learned was from a publican. During the early hours of one morning, the man was asleep in one of the bedrooms upstairs when he heard the sound of small pebbles hitting the window. It didn't cause him any alarm as it had happened in the past, and he knew who to expect outside. He said that he was grinning to himself in a happy way as he walked towards the window, and when he looked outside, he saw Bobby and his friends standing there, looking upwards from below the window. The man had already picked up his door keys, which he dropped down to Bobby so that he could let himself in. The man told me that he then closed the window and returned to his bed. When he woke the next morning, he went downstairs to a silent, empty saloon. It looked like it did on any other morning, tidy and ready for opening. There weren't any obvious signs that people had been enjoying a few drinks, except for the pound notes that had been left on the bar to pay for all that had been consumed.

I remember a time when I was walking from one site to the next in the city to carry out daily maintenance checks when I encountered another engineer who worked for the same company as me. I noticed that we were wearing the same uniform, but he was completely unknown to me. He stopped me in the street and we started a friendly conversation. The man told me about a time when he had worked at Wembley Stadium. He said that he was on duty during the big matches and that he sometimes met the football players. On one occasion, Bobby Moore and a couple of other people were at the back of the stadium at the same time as him. The engineer said that Bobby had the capability to make everyone laugh with his humour and that he had a great character.

On another occasion, I was working in a guy's kitchen doing a boiler repair. I had taken my dog, Dolly, along with me to the job. I hadn't had her for very long. The man had a lovely house which felt homely and welcoming. It was a warm, summer's day. Dolly played with the man's dog in the back garden whilst I worked on the boiler. The dogs got along well together. I could tell that the man had a lot of love for his family. He had his young grandchild in his arms and I could see how proud he and his wife were, as I am of my grandchildren. My mobile phone was on the worktop above me. I asked the man if he wanted to see a picture of my grandchildren and he said yes. The man immediately commented about my grandson's similarities to me. It made me happy to hear that. I then told them how much I look like my father and showed them another picture that I had on my phone. The man's wife looked at the picture in pure astonishment. Her mouth dropped right open. I was at this point that I discovered the man used to be a professional football player and that he had known Bobby Moore well. We both went into the dining room area where the man told me about my dad and how he had helped him with his game. He told me that my dad had been a great character. It was a happy encounter, and we talked for quite some time. Both of us were equally pleased to meet the other.

These are just a few recollections of conversations that I had with strangers about my dad. I enjoyed and appreciated hearing about every one of them as they brought me closer to the man that I never really knew. They enabled me to build up a picture in my mind, and I was glad to learn that everyone had good memories of him, especially when they all said that he was so likeable. Not a bad word was said against him.

I grew up with a step-father that I hated, rather than my true biological father, someone that I had to call dad. From the day of my birth, I was without a father so I didn't know what it was like to have one in my life. I never missed what I never had when I was very young. However, I watched my two sisters and other kids with their dads over the years, being with both parents, interacting with them. They had their dads watching them play sports and enjoyed sports activities together as well as getting all of the confidence that they needed to do well in life. Other kids got help with their homework and important decisions as they went into adulthood. But there was no help for me. It made me feel like I'd been robbed. I gradually realised what I had missed out on. I would have liked the same kind of life, to have a father there encouraging me and acting proud. I would have liked to have a father that I could look up to and share the joy of achievements with.

Mum always said that I was special and that I would have no worries when I got older. Other members of my family, my sisters Ann and Clair, even Tina said so in a roundabout way many years later. However, their predictions were very far from the truth. I have done everything for myself. I don't know why I was never properly acknowledged or supported by my father. Looking back, Mum's life also changed dramatically at the time that the affair came out and she paid for it for the rest of her life. Mum could no longer go to see her father, or ask for financial support from him. She was completely reliant on David. When he abused us, she couldn't just get up and walk out. When Grandad came and took me away, I imagine that she felt like she had lost everything. That must have really hurt her, and I am sure that this episode in our lives affected her mental health in a negative way.

I asked Mum about my father quite a few times throughout my life. She was always quite vague, but she did tell me that he had a red sports car. On one occasion, Mum asked me if I remembered the big teddy that I had when I was a baby. It had pride of place on the top of my bed until I was seven years old. She said to me, "Your father gave you that teddy the day you were born." Mum said that he brought it to the hospital and gave it to me. In previous conversations, she just shrugged my existence off as a one night stand. But I realised that couldn't be true if he was there at my birth.

I found it extremely frustrating that Mum wouldn't tell me who my father was. My aunt and other family members knew as well, and even though I tried to trick them into letting it slip out, they never did. I believe that everyone ought to know who their parents are. It's not fair for families to keep secrets. People who know both of their parents have no idea what it's like not to know their history or where they came from. I didn't think about that at all as a young boy. However, as I grew older, it became increasingly more important to me. I wondered if my father and I shared the same mannerisms. Did I look or sound like him? Did we share the same interests? These are things that most people take for granted yet I didn't have the privilege of knowing until much later on.

I never realised that my biological father had watched me growing up from a distance until it was too late, or that we had been in each other's company more than I ever could have imagined. Even though it is too late for me to meet him in person as his son, I have always felt fortunate that I have been able to learn about Bobby by reading his own words in books, watching the many video recordings that are available on the internet. I appreciate that the majority of people do not have that opportunity, and I am grateful that I have these resources available to me.

I have only known who my father is since 2012. It took two major losses in my life, only one year apart, for the seeds of truth to be sown and for realisation to follow. I'm now seeking closure in this part of my life. By writing this book, I have explained my journey with the highs and the lows that I have encountered along the way. I feel fortunate that I have been able to use the World Wide Web to see what kind of man he was, to hear his voice, to listen to people's stories about him and to learn how revered and admired he was on and off of the pitch.

Final Thoughts

When I think about my journey, I can see in hindsight that I've been seeking the truth for many years. The holiday to Spain with Terrie was the first time that I really started to challenge everything that I thought to be true. If I was lied to about the name of a place I went to as a child, what else was a lie? What were people trying to hide and why was it so important to keep secrets from me?

I have lived a life, but people who have listened about my past say that I should have had a better life. I didn't mind the rough and tumble as it moulded me into the person that I am and helped me to deal with the curve balls that life has thrown at me. It doesn't bother me that I grew up without the luxuries that I could have had if I'd been raised as Bobby's child. It does bother me a great deal that I grew up with David and his abusive ways. The realisation that I was denied the love of other family members hurt me. Especially when I remember how good it was to be in their company as a child. We shared some great times together, that I now feel I was only able to enjoy because I'm Bobby's son. Why else would I have gone on extravagant holidays abroad and stayed in a mansion? They're not the kind of things that a typical South London child got up to.

On the whole, I have been accurate with my version of events, despite them happening around five decades ago. But I have to admit that they haven't always been exactly right. When I've researched for facts, I've either been spot on or very close. For instance, I knew the name of the woman who won the Miss World contest that I attended with Mum and Bobby. I thought that it was in 1970. But when I did a Google search, I learned that Eva Rueber-Staier won the contest in 1969. However, these are only minor discrepancies and overall my account of events has been very accurate.

Some people have asked me why I wanted to go to the trouble of telling my story in a book. It has been difficult to make sense of all of the memories and

186

conversations that I have had about Bobby without writing them down and ordering them. This did take a great deal of effort as I have never attempted anything like it before. I had considered writing a book about my journey for around five years before I actually started to put pen to paper in a purposeful way. I conducted a lot of research during that period, even hiring a professional genealogist. I needed that time to figure out who the people in the photographs that my aunt left me were and decipher the truths from the untruths.

The book writing process took less than two years from start to finish; however, it has required many hours of input. This was mostly made possible by the Coronavirus pandemic. Being unable to go out to work gave me the opportunity to sit down and concentrate hard, writing almost daily. I very quickly realised that I needed my notes processed into something resembling book form. I believe that there are certain times when people come along to help us get through our lives. By April 2020, I had written forty pages, but I had no means of transferring my work into digital form. I asked a good friend if they knew anyone locally that could assist me. That's when Nichola Robinson and her family came into my life. She has put a great deal of her own time into working with me on my manuscript and, between us, we have got the job done. Without her input, I would not have managed to complete it. I would like to take this opportunity to thank Nichola and her family from the bottom of my heart.

The writing became much easier as time went on. It felt like a monstrous task at times, and I was not confident that I could come up with enough relatable content to fill a whole book. However, I shouldn't have worried about that because I've realised that much of the events in my life have been relevant to my intended audience. Forgotten memories and thoughts are still coming back to me, and I have had to return to my writing several times to add the revived memories to my story. Making sense of those memories helped me to understand why certain events took place in my life, too.

It has been a very up-and-down experience. There were days where I felt quite accomplished and positive. Yet there have been other days where thinking about putting the bad memories onto paper made me feel really low. I experienced the shakes and terrible anxiety. I went into my own shell and avoided other people, even when I was out walking my loyal companion, Dolly Drop. The process of writing itself has been utterly transformative, almost like therapy. It has forced me to revisit the most emotionally challenging times in my life and to think about them more subjectively. The burden that I have carried for so many years has been offloaded and I feel lighter, calmer and more content than ever before.

Other people have asked me what it is that I want out of this. It's not an easy thing, telling your life story to the world, opening old wounds and setting yourself up for public scrutiny. It feels a bit like selling your soul to the devil. I usually keep my thoughts to myself. It's never been my style to tell-all. So it's been hard to write about certain people, especially when I've known that it will undoubtedly cause others to think differently of them. But then I reminded myself that none of this has ever been my fault. I didn't ask for any of this to happen and I do deserve the truth.

Despite the deception that I have experienced, I don't wish to hold grudges. Family members have lied to me so much that it must have become easier to keep the pretence up rather than admit that they had been lying to my face all along. Publishing a book about my life has never been about hurting people or exacting some kind of revenge. I needed to do it for me, for my children and for my children's children. It's their history too and I owe it to them to put things right. I've never had a wish to change the past, and I'm not expecting this to make a great deal of difference to my future. I suppose the most important thing to me is recognition. I want to be able to say that Bobby Moore is my father.